Sew the Perfect Gift

25 Handmade Projects from Top Designers

Martingale®
& COMPANY

Sew the Perfect Gift: 25 Handmade Projects from Top Designers
© 2011 by Martingale & Company

That Patchwork Place® is an imprint of Martingale & Company®.

Martingale & Company
19021 120th Ave. NE, Ste. 102
Bothell, WA 98011-9511 USA
www.martingale-pub.com

Printed in China
16 15 14 13 12 11   8 7 6 5 4 3 2 1

Library of Congress Cataloging-in-Publication Data is available upon request.

ISBN: 978-1-60468-069-0

Mission Statement
Dedicated to providing quality products and service to inspire creativity.

Credits
President & CEO: Tom Wierzbicki
Editor in Chief: Mary V. Green
Managing Editor: Karen Costello Soltys
Technical Editor: Ellen Pahl
Copy Editor: Liz McGehee
Design Director: Stan Green
Production Manager: Regina Girard
Illustrator: Laurel Strand
Cover & Text Designer: Adrienne Smitke
Photographer: Brent Kane

Special thanks to Pier 1 Imports for generously providing props for this book.

Contents

Giving Just Got a Lot More Fun

"I love it!" How rewarding it is to give a beautiful gift to someone we care about—especially when the treasure is our own handiwork. And how happy it makes the recipient! *Sew the Perfect Gift* offers an assortment of exciting designs that you'll be absolutely tickled to give to your family and friends throughout the year.

Choose from eye-catching projects in styles ranging from traditional to a little bit zany. Rub creative shoulders with such talented designers as Linda Lum DeBono, Kim Brackett, Kim Diehl, and Avis Shirer. And be well prepared for every gift occasion, with projects ranging from Christmas to home decor to specialty items for knitters, thrifters, travelers, and more.

Get Wise to Wool

If you've never worked with wool, you're in for a treat. Discover how pleasurable it is to incorporate wool appliqué into your projects. Now you can make such charming items as Harvest Bouquet Candle Mat (page 6), Plum Purple Pillow (page 22), Heartfelt Journal (page 53), and Squarely in the Round Wool Bracelets (page 92). To get started, find helpful hints about felting wool on page 107.

Go Green

You'll discover clever ways to thrift it and gift it with the projects in "It's Easy to Be Green," beginning on page 72. Put that well-loved denim to a great new use as a fabulous Dungaree Denim Scarf (page 72). Or upcycle the wool from a thrift-store sweater into the Recycled-Wool Wristlet Purse and Companion Cup Cozy (page 77). Give someone a break—an eco-friendly lunch break—with Lunch-Break Reusable Bags (page 82). There's even more to explore in this inspiring chapter, so check it out.

Browse the Basics

Most of the projects in *Sew the Perfect Gift* are relatively easy to complete. We've included step-by-step instructions and illustrations so that the gifts are as fun to make as they are to give. We've also provided an illustrated glossary in "Basic Sewing Techniques—An Illustrated Glossary," beginning on page 105. If you run across any sewing terms you're unfamiliar with, just flip to this section for instant help.

Begin!

Delight in the wonderful colors, textures, and styles you'll explore as you create each gorgeous gift. Then enjoy giving a thing of beauty to those you love—and that includes, of course, yourself!

Harvest Bouquet Candle Mat

Designed and made by Kim Diehl

This small quilt will fit the bill for anyone who loves both patchwork and appliqué. It has lots of pint-size charm and won't take long to make. It includes quilting cottons in fat eighths, fat quarters, and charm squares and luscious bits of wool for the appliqués. Who could ask for anything more?

~Kim

Finished size: 22½" x 22½" ❁ **Finished block: 4" x 4"**

Materials

Yardage is based on 42"-wide fabric.

2 fat quarters of brown print for sashing strips
    and binding
1 fat quarter of tan print for blocks and sashing
    corner squares
1 fat quarter of orange print for border
9 charm squares (5" x 5") of assorted prints for blocks
4 squares, 3½" x 3½", of assorted prints for border
    corner squares
1 fat eighth of dark green plaid for vines
8 rectangles, 3" x 4", of assorted felted wool for
    tulip appliqués
8 squares, 2" x 2", of assorted felted wool for tulip-
    petal appliqués
Scraps of assorted green felted wool for leaf appliqués
¾ yard of fabric for backing
27" x 27" piece of batting
½ yard of lightweight 18"-wide fusible web
¼" bias bar
Liquid fabric glue
Size 8 or 12 pearl cotton in a neutral color for wool
    appliqués and hand quilting
Size 5 embroidery needle
Fine-gauge thread for stitching dark green plaid stems
Appliqué needle
Seam ripper

Cutting

From the tan print, cut:
9 squares, 2⅞" x 2⅞"; cut each square in half
    diagonally to yield 18 triangles
18 squares, 1⅞" x 1⅞"; cut each square in half
    diagonally to yield 36 triangles
52 squares, 1½" x 1½"

From each assorted-print charm square, cut:*
1 square, 2⅞" x 2⅞"; cut the square in half
    diagonally to yield 2 triangles (18 total)
2 squares, 1⅞" x 1⅞"; cut each square in half
    diagonally to yield 4 triangles (36 total)

From one brown print fat quarter, cut:
24 rectangles, 1½" x 4½"

From the second brown print fat quarter, cut:
5 binding strips, 2½" x 22"

From the orange print, cut:
4 rectangles, 3½" x 16½"

From the dark green plaid, cut on the bias:
8 rectangles, 1" x 8"

**Keep the patchwork pieces separated by print
to simplify the piecing process.*

Piecing the Blocks

1. Select a set of matching patchwork pieces cut from one assorted-print charm square. Join a tan print $2\frac{7}{8}$" triangle with an assorted print $2\frac{7}{8}$" triangle, stitching along the long diagonal edges. Press the seam allowances toward the assorted print. Trim away the dog-ear points. Repeat to make two large half-square-triangle units. ①

2. Repeat step 1 using four tan print $1\frac{7}{8}$" triangles and four assorted-print $1\frac{7}{8}$" triangles to make four small half-square-triangle units.

3. Lay out two small half-square-triangle units and two tan print $1\frac{1}{2}$" squares as shown. Join the pieces in each horizontal row. Press the seam allowances toward the tan print. Join the rows. Press the seam allowances to one side. Repeat to make two pieced units. ②

4. Lay out two large half-square-triangle units and two units from step 3 as shown. Join the units in each horizontal row. Press the seam allowances toward the large half-square-triangle units. Join the rows. Press the seam allowances to one side. ③

5. Repeat steps 1–4 to make nine pieced blocks measuring $4\frac{1}{2}$" square, including the seam allowances.

Assembling the Quilt Top

1. Lay out four tan print $1\frac{1}{2}$" squares and three brown print $1\frac{1}{2}$" x $4\frac{1}{2}$" rectangles, alternating them as shown. Join the pieces. Press the seam allowances toward the brown print. Repeat to make four sashing rows. ④

2. Lay out four brown print $1\frac{1}{2}$" x $4\frac{1}{2}$" rectangles and three pieced blocks, alternating them as shown. Join the pieces. Press the seam allowances toward the brown print. Repeat to make three block rows. ⑤

3. Referring to the quilt photo, lay out the sashing rows and the block rows to form the quilt center. Join the rows. Press the seam allowances toward the sashing rows.

4. Join an orange print $3\frac{1}{2}$" x $16\frac{1}{2}$" rectangle to the right and left sides of the quilt center. Press the seam allowances toward the orange print. Join an assorted-print $3\frac{1}{2}$" square to each end of the remaining orange print $3\frac{1}{2}$" x $16\frac{1}{2}$" rectangles. Press the seam allowances toward the orange print. Join these pieced rectangles to the remaining sides of the quilt center. Press the seam allowances toward the orange print. The quilt top should now measure $22\frac{1}{2}$" square, including the seam allowances.

Preparing the Stems

1. With wrong sides together, fold each dark green plaid 1" x 8" rectangle in half lengthwise and use a scant $\frac{1}{4}$" seam allowance to stitch along the long raw edges to form a tube. Slide the bias bar through each tube to easily press it flat, centering the seam allowance so that it will be hidden from the front of the finished stem. (If the seam allowance will be visible, trim it to $\frac{1}{8}$".) ⑥

2. Place small dots of liquid fabric glue along the seam line underneath the pressed seam allowance at approximately ½" to 1" intervals. Use a hot, dry iron on the wrong side of the stem to heat-set the glue and fuse the seams in place.

Preparing the Wool Appliqués

Please refer to page 10 for the appliqué pattern pieces.

1. Trace the following appliqué shapes the number of times indicated onto the paper-backing side of the fusible web, leaving approximately ½" between each shape:

    - 8 of pattern A
    - 24 of pattern B
    - 26 of pattern C

2. Cut out each shape approximately ¼" *outside* the drawn line; then cut away the center portion of the shape approximately ¼" *inside* the drawn lines (this will eliminate bulk and keep the appliqués soft and pliable after they've been stitched). It isn't necessary to cut away the centers of the B shapes because of their small size.

3. Following the manufacturer's instructions, fuse a prepared A shape, paper side up, to each 3" x 4" rectangle of wool. Repeat with the prepared B shapes, placing three B pieces onto each 2" square of wool. Fuse the prepared C shapes onto scraps of assorted green wool. Cut out each shape exactly on the drawn lines.

Stitching the Appliqués

1. Select a prepared A appliqué and a set of three matching B appliqués. Remove the paper backing from the B appliqués only. Place small dots of liquid fabric glue around the perimeter of each B piece and position them onto the A appliqué. Use a hot, dry iron to heat-set the glue and fuse the layers together from the front. Repeat with the remaining A and B appliqués.

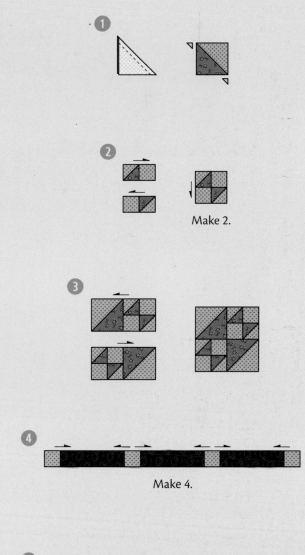

Make 2.

Make 4.

Make 3.

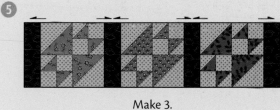

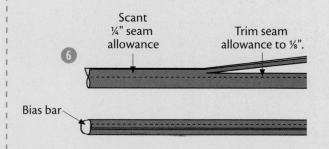

Scant ¼" seam allowance

Trim seam allowance to ⅛".

Bias bar

Wool Appliqué Made Easy

The combination of fusible adhesive and the liquid glue produces ideal results because the iron-on adhesive finishes and stabilizes the underside of the wool edges to reduce fraying, while the glue-basted edges hold the layers of wool together beautifully for easy stitching without pinning.

2. Use pearl cotton and a size 5 embroidery needle to stitch the appliqués in place. Kim likes to stitch her appliqués using an overhand stitch or whipstitch rather than the traditional blanket stitch. Refer to "Blanket Stitch" on page 106 for additional details if needed. Tie off and knot the threads from the back.

3. Referring to the quilt photo, use a seam ripper to open a 1½"-wide area of two opposing corner blocks to insert the stems.

4. Remove the paper backing from all remaining appliqués. Using the quilt photo as a guide, position four prepared tulip appliqués onto the quilt top; pin in place. Lay out three prepared stems, tucking the raw ends into the open patchwork seam at least ¼" and curving them to join the tulips, again tucking under at least ¼". Trim away any excess stem length to achieve the look you desire. Place small dots of liquid glue underneath the stems at approximately ½" to 1" intervals to anchor them in place. Position and glue-baste a fourth stem to connect the final tulip to the original portion of the design. Apply small dots of liquid fabric glue to the adhesive area of 14 leaves and position them along the stems as desired. Heat-set the appliqués and stems from the back of the quilt top.

5. Use a needle and thread to hand stitch the patchwork opening, sewing along the original seam line.

6. Using a fine-gauge thread to match the dark green plaid and an appliqué needle, stitch the stems to the quilt top. Use pearl cotton and a size 5 embroidery needle to stitch the wool appliqués in place.

7. Repeat steps 3–6 to complete the appliqué design on the opposite corner of the quilt top.

Completing the Quilt

1. Layer the quilt top, batting, and backing; baste the layers together.

2. Quilt the layers. The featured quilt was hand quilted in the big-stitch method with the blocks quilted "in the ditch" (along the seam lines); the long diagonal block seams were also stitched ¼" away on each side of the seams. Large Xs were quilted onto the brown sashing strips, and Xs were stitched onto all corner squares. The border was stitched with alternating wide and narrow lines to fill the open background areas, and the appliqués were outlined.

3. Join the five brown print 2½" x 22" strips into one length and use it to bind the quilt. Refer to "Binding" on page 105.

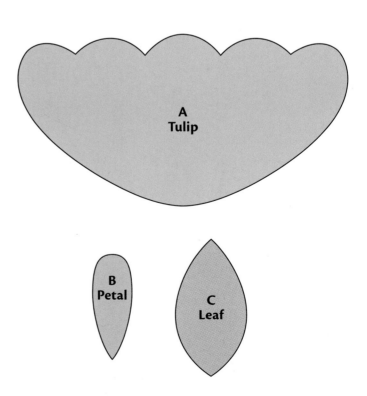

A
Tulip

B
Petal

C
Leaf

Tiny Table Topper

Designed and made by Kim Brackett

Use your tiniest scraps and strip piecing to make this sweet table topper. All you need are several bright 1½" x 10½" strips, a solid for the block backgrounds, and four fun coordinating prints for the borders. You'll use up some of your stash and have an unforgettable gift for a special friend or family member.

~Kim

Finished quilt: 19½" x 19½" ❈ Finished block: 3" x 3"

Materials

Yardage is based on 42"-wide fabric.

⅝ yard *total* of assorted print scraps for blocks
    and borders
½ yard of off-white solid fabric for block backgrounds
¼ yard of red polka-dot fabric for binding
¾ yard of fabric for backing
24" x 24" piece of batting

Cutting

From the off-white solid, cut:
7 strips, 1½" x 42"; crosscut into:
    25 strips, 1½" x 10½"

From the assorted prints, cut:
2 border strips, 2½" x 15½"
2 border strips, 2½" x 19½"
25 strips, 1½" x 10½"

From the red polka-dot fabric, cut:
3 binding strips, 2½" x 42"

Making the Blocks

1. Sew together a print 1½" x 10½" strip and an off-white 1½" x 10½" strip, long sides together, as shown. Press the seam allowances toward the print strip. Sew 25 strip sets. ①

2. Photocopy or trace the template pattern on page 13. Cut out the template around the outside edges. It should be 2" square. Tape the template, right side up, to the bottom of a 6" square ruler (or any ruler with a 2" mark). Place the ruler on the pair of sewn strips so that the line in the middle of the template follows the seam line on the pair of strips. Cut along the right and top edges of the ruler. Rotate the cut piece to trim the edges as shown, placing the previously cut edges along the edge of the template. Cut along the right and top edges of the ruler. Continue cutting units until you've cut four from each strip set.

3. Using the four units cut in step 2, construct the blocks as shown. Press the seam allowances in a counterclockwise direction. Make 25 blocks. ③

Assembling the Quilt Top

1. Arrange the blocks in five horizontal rows of five blocks each. Sew the blocks together in rows, pressing the seam allowances in alternating directions from row to row. Sew the rows together. Press the seam allowances in the same direction. ④
2. Add the 2½" x 15½" side borders as shown. Press the seam allowances toward the border strips.
3. Sew the 2½" x 19½" bottom and top border strips to the quilt and press the seam allowances toward the border strips. ⑤

Completing the Quilt

1. Layer the quilt top, batting, and backing; baste the layers together.
2. Quilt as desired.
3. Join the three red polka-dot strips into one length and use it to bind the quilt. Refer to "Binding" on page 105.

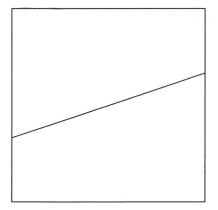

Cutting template pattern

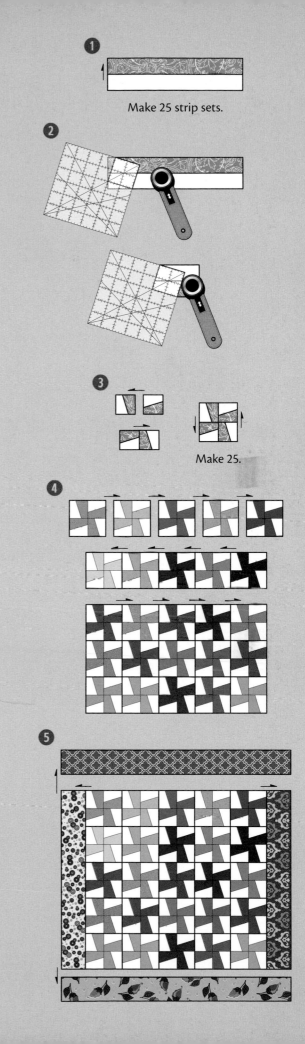

Make 25 strip sets.

Make 25.

Time for Tea, Have a Cup with Me

Designed and made by Kay Mackenzie

Gather fabrics and buttons in your pal's favorite colors. She's sure to love this little quilt, especially if you include it with a gift of your time: sit down, brew a pot of tea, and have a long chat when you give it to her!

~Kay

❀ **Finished size: 14" x 9"** ❀

Materials

Yardage is based on 42"-wide fabric.

1 fat eighth of white polka-dot fabric for wall background

1 fat eighth or ⅛ yard of blue print for table background, clock, and spoon holder

8" x 10" piece of red print 1 for teapot and teacups

4" x 6" piece of red print 2 for teacups, saucers, and teapot lid

4" x 8" piece of white solid for clock face

Scrap of light blue print for spoons

Scrap of green print for leaves

¼ yard of red print 3 for binding

1 fat quarter of fabric for backing

11" x 16" piece of batting

½ yard of 18"-wide paper-backed fusible web

Nonstick appliqué pressing sheet

Threads for machine appliqué

Fine-point permanent fabric marker or embroidery thread for clock hands

Buttons (sizes are approximate)

- 4 buttons, ¼" diameter, for spoon rack
- 12 buttons, ⅜" diameter, for clock face
- 1 button, ½" diameter, for teapot flower center
- 2 buttons, ¾" to 1" diameter, for clock center and teapot lid

19 buttons for back of quilt (optional)

12" of rickrack for hanging (optional)

Cutting

From the white polka-dot fabric, cut:

1 rectangle, 7½" x 15"

From the blue print, cut:

1 rectangle, 3" x 15"

From red print 3, cut:

2 strips, 2½" x 42"

Preparing the Appliqués

Refer to "Fusible Appliqué" on page 108. The appliqué patterns are on page 17 and are reversed for fusible appliqué. Cut away the centers of the teapot and teacup fusible-web shapes before fusing to the fabrics. The clock-face circles do not need any fusible web, as the blue clock rim will anchor them.

From the blue print, cut:

1 clock rim

1 spoon holder

From red print 1, cut:

1 *each* of teapot, spout, and handle

2 *each* of teacups and teacup handles

From red print 2, cut:

2 *each* of teacup interior and saucer

1 teapot lid

1 flower for teapot

From the white solid, cut:

2 clock-face circles (using the dashed circle)

From the light blue print, cut:

2 spoons

From the green print, cut:

2 leaves

Avoid Show-Through on Light Fabrics

If you're using light fabrics as Kay did for the teapot lid and saucers, you can avoid darker fabrics showing through by using a double layer of light fabric for those pieces. First fuse two layers of fabric together and then use this fused fabric for the motifs.

Assembling the Quilt

1. Sew the blue print 3" x 15" rectangle to the polka-dot 7½" x 15" rectangle using a ¼" seam. Press seam allowances toward the blue print. The background is slightly oversized and will be trimmed after the quilting is done. ①

2. Center one white clock-face circle, right side up, over the dashed circle template. Trace the clock hands and button placement onto the fabric.

3. Remove the paper backing from the fused motifs and compose each unit on a nonstick appliqué pressing sheet. Lightly adhere the pieces together with a warm, dry iron.

4. Arrange the units on the background, referring to the photograph on page 14 for placement guidance. Layer the two clock-face circles, with the unmarked circle underneath, to prevent shadow-through. Place the blue clock rim over the clock face. Fuse all elements in place. Stitch by machine, using a blanket stitch, zigzag, or other stitch.

5. Cut away the background and the seam behind the teapot and teacups, leaving at least a ¼" seam allowance all around. This will prevent the seam allowance from creating a ridge in the finished appliqués. ②

6. Layer the quilt top with batting and backing and quilt as you like. (Remember that the project is still slightly oversized.) Sew buttons in place through all layers.

When she stitched the buttons on the front, Kay sewed opposing buttons on the back of the quilt at the same time, to hide the knots.

Completing the Quilt

1. Trim the quilt to 14" x 9".
2. Use the red print 3 strips to bind the quilt, referring to "Binding" on page 105.
3. Attach a label, add a hanging sleeve or a rickrack hanger, and give to your teatime friend!

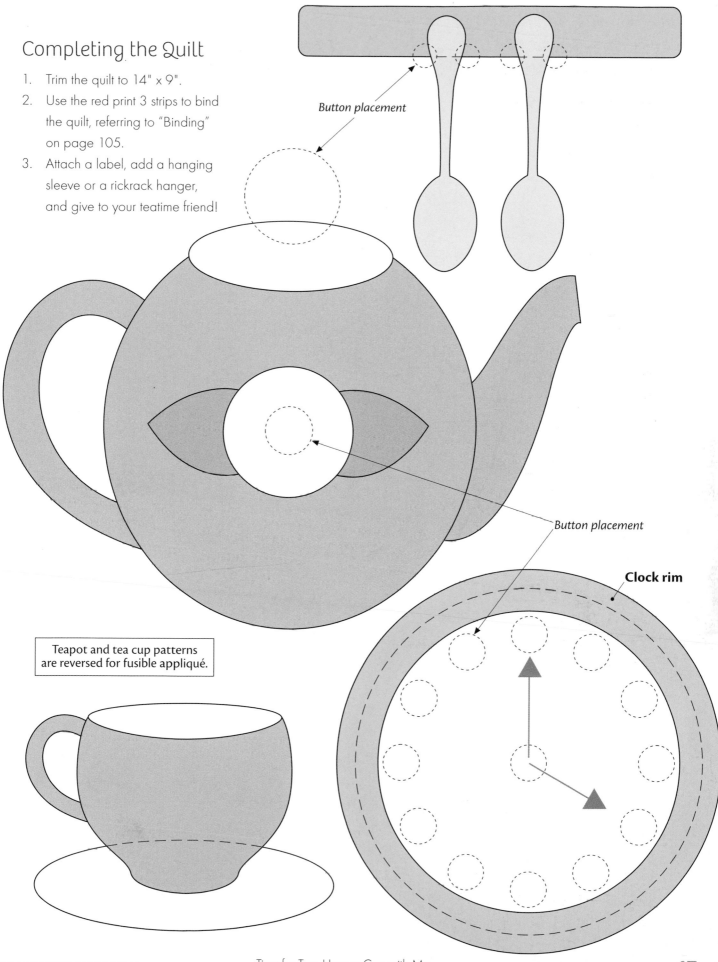

Button placement

Button placement

Clock rim

Teapot and tea cup patterns are reversed for fusible appliqué.

Totally Taupe Table Runner

Designed and made by Mary V. Green; machine quilted by Krista Moser

This easy table runner would look great in almost any fabric combination. I wanted a seasonless look that would work well in my friend's neutral-toned dining room. I used a collection of fat quarters of Japanese taupe fabrics that I'd been saving for just the right project.

~Mary

Finished table runner: 17" x 57" ❁ Finished block: 4½" x 4½"

Materials

Yardage is based on 42"-wide fabric.

1 yard *total* of assorted light and medium prints for block backgrounds and appliqués

½ yard *total* of assorted medium and dark prints for appliqués

½ yard *total* of medium prints for border

⅜ yard of fabric for binding

1⅛ yards of fabric for backing

23" x 62" piece of batting

1 yard of 18"-wide fusible web (optional)

Precuts Make It Fast!

You can easily make this table runner using Layer Cakes (10" x 10" squares) and charm squares (5" x 5" squares). With most of the cutting already done, you can get to the sewing faster!

Cutting

From the assorted light and medium prints, cut:

6 squares, 10" x 10"; cut in half diagonally to yield 12 triangles. You will use only 6 of them.*

16 squares, 5" x 5"

* Mary used six different prints. If you prefer, cut three squares, cut each in half diagonally, and use both triangles from each square.

From the medium prints for border, cut:**

2 strips, 2½" x 42"

2 strips, 2½" x 16"

2 strips, 2½" x 14"

From the binding fabric, cut:

4 strips, 2" x 42"

** If you use fat quarters, piece strips on the diagonal to get the length needed. For each end, you will need one 14"-long strip and one matching 16"-long strip.

Making the Blocks

Use your favorite appliqué technique to prepare the circle appliqués.

1. Prepare 16 circles using template A and the medium and dark prints. Prepare 2 half circles using template B and medium and dark prints. Prepare 4 half circles using template B and the light and medium prints.

2. Select a 5" background square for each circle. To center a circle on a background square, fold each square into quarters and lightly finger-press the folds. Fold the circle into quarters and lightly finger-press the folds. Unfold the pieces. Push a pin through the center point of the circle and into the center point of the square. Align the creases on the two pieces, remove the pin, and pin or fuse the circle appliqué to the square. Stitch around the edges of the appliqué by hand or machine using a blanket stitch or invisible machine stitch. Repeat to make 16 blocks.

3. Select a background triangle for each half-circle appliqué. To position a half circle on a triangle, fold it in half and lightly finger-press the fold. Fold the triangle in half and lightly finger-press. Handle these triangles carefully, as the long edge is on the bias and will stretch easily. Unfold the pieces and place the half circle on the triangle as shown, aligning the creases and the straight edges. Pin or fuse the appliqué to the triangle and stitch as before. Repeat to make six side triangles. ①

Assembling the Table Runner

1. Referring to the quilt-assembly diagram below, arrange the blocks and setting triangles on a design wall, table, or floor. When you're pleased with the arrangement, sew each grouping of four 5" squares together to make a Four Patch block. Make four blocks. ②

2. Sew the blocks and side triangles together in diagonal rows as shown. Handle the triangles carefully; the long edges are on the bias and will stretch easily. Press as indicated. Sew the rows together and press the seam allowances in one direction. ③

3. Use a rotary cutter and ruler to trim and even up the triangles along the long edges of the quilt top, making sure to leave a ¼" seam allowance where they are joined to the Four Patch blocks. ④

Adding the Borders

1. Fold the 2½" x 42" border strips in half crosswise and finger-press the center point. Fold the quilt top in half and finger-press the center point of the long edges. With right sides together and matching center points, pin and sew a border to each long edge of the quilt top. Press the seam allowances toward the borders. Trim the ends even with the edge of the quilt top as shown. ⑤

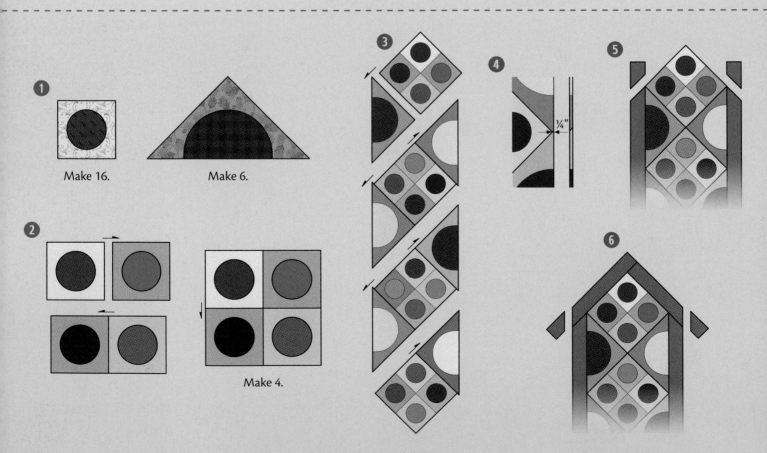

Make 16. Make 6.

Make 4.

¼"

2. Sew a 2½" x 14" strip to the right edge of one pointed end of the quilt top; press. Trim the ends even with the quilt top. Sew a matching 2½" x 16" strip to the left edge. Press and trim. ⑥

3. Repeat step 2 to sew the remaining strips to the opposite end of the quilt top. Press and trim.

Completing the Table Runner

Layer the quilt top with the batting and backing; baste the layers together. Follow the quilting suggestion below or quilt as desired. Bind the edges with the 2"-wide binding strips, referring to "Binding" on page 105. ⑦

⑦

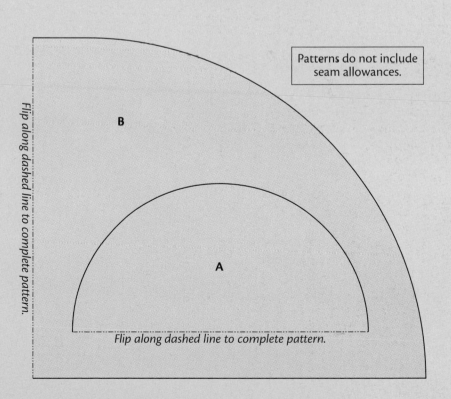

Patterns do not include seam allowances.

B

A

Flip along dashed line to complete pattern.

Flip along dashed line to complete pattern.

Plum Purple Pillow

Designed and made by Jeanne Large and Shelley Wicks

This pillow will be a cheerful accent and comfy addition to any room of the house! The row of perky daisies and double rows of rickrack are sure to make you—and your friends—smile.

~Jeanne & Shelley

❀ **Finished size: 30" x 18"** ❀

Materials

Yardage is based on 42"-wide fabric.

1 yard of ivory tone-on-tone print for pillow top and back

⅜ yard of brown print for pillow top

4 squares, 5½" x 5½", of felted wool in various shades of purple for daisies

2½" x 10" piece of brown felted wool for daisy centers

1¾ yards of ½"-wide beige rickrack

4 ivory ½"-diameter buttons

3 brown ¾"-diameter buttons

2 pieces of batting, 20" x 32"

½ yard of 18"-wide fusible web

32 ounces of fiberfill stuffing*

*Another option is to do what Jeanne and Shelley usually do: purchase a regular bed-size pillow, open it, and use the stuffing from that.

Cutting

From the ivory print, cut:

1 rectangle, 8½" x 30½"

1 piece, 20" x 32"

From the brown print, cut:

1 rectangle, 10½" x 30½"

Piecing and Quilting the Pillow

1. Sew the 8½" x 30½" ivory rectangle to the 10½" x 30½" brown rectangle along the long edges to make the pillow top. Press the seam allowance toward the brown fabric. ①

2. Layer the pillow top on top of one of the pieces of batting with right side up and baste or pin the layers together. (You may use a piece of muslin on the back if you plan to do hand quilting; the fabric will be on the inside of the pillow and will not be seen.) Quilt the pillow top with an allover design, such as the loop pattern shown. Trim the excess batting even with the edges of the pillow top. Repeat with the 20" x 32" ivory piece and the remaining piece of batting. Trim to the same size as the pillow top. ②

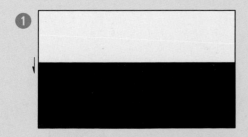

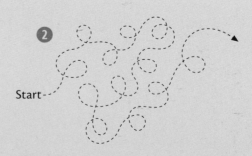

Start

Appliquéing the Pillow

1. Using the patterns on below, trace four daisies and four flower centers onto the paper side of the fusible web. Cut out each piece, leaving ½" around each shape. Press the flower shapes onto the purple felted wool squares, and the flower centers onto the brown felted wool piece, following the manufacturer's instructions. Cut out directly on the drawn line and peel off the paper backing.

2. Using the photo on page 22 as a guide, place the daisies on the ivory section of the pillow top approximately 2" apart and ¼" above the brown seam line. Allow the extra space to be evenly distributed at the two outside edges (approximately 3½" on each side). When the pillow is stuffed, the extra space won't be noticeable, and the daisies will be nicely centered on the front.

3. Following the manufacturer's instructions for the fusible web, press the daisies and flower centers in place. Stitch around each shape by hand or machine using a blanket stitch.

4. Sew a brown button between each daisy. Sew an ivory button on each flower center.

5. Position the rickrack on the brown fabric, 1" from the seam line. Pin in place. Position the second row of rickrack 2¼" from the seam line and pin in place. Sew a straight line through the center of each length of rickrack.

Tips for Fusing Wool

- Be sure to read the instructions carefully for the fusible product you're using. Too hot an iron can scorch the wool.
- If you find it difficult to fuse the wool appliqué shape to the cotton background fabric, try pinning in place, flipping the project over, and pressing well from the back. The heat will easily penetrate the cotton, melt the glue, and fuse down your wool shape.
- When layering wool appliqué shapes, it works best to fuse one layer at a time.

Completing the Pillow

1. Lay the pillow front on top of the pillow back with right sides together and pin. Sew around the outside edges using a ¼" seam allowance and leaving a 6" opening along the bottom of the pillow. ③

2. Turn the pillow right side out, pushing the corners out with your fingers or the blunt end of a pencil. Stuff the pillow with the fiberfill and sew the opening closed by hand.

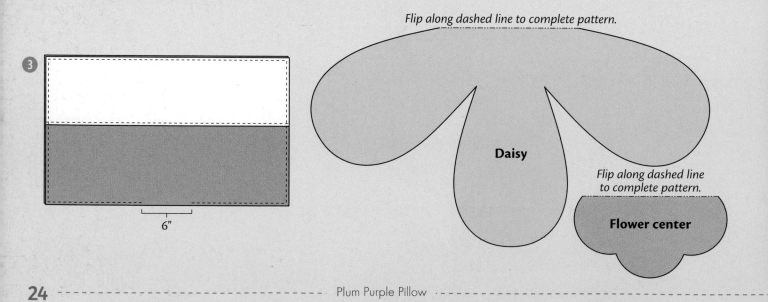

Flip along dashed line to complete pattern.

6"

Daisy

Flip along dashed line to complete pattern.

Flower center

Wheat-Stalk Throw Pillow

Designed and made by Vanessa Christenson

This is a fast and super-easy craft to decorate your home or to give as a housewarming gift to a new homeowner. The possibilities are endless for the holidays as well; you can easily make a stencil for whatever the occasion!

~Vanessa

❀ **Finished size: 17½" x 11½"** ❀

Materials

Yardage is based on 42"-wide fabric.

½ yard of muslin for pillow
Krylon spray paint in brown (or color of choice)
Freezer paper
32 ounces of fiberfill stuffing

Cutting

From the muslin, cut:

2 rectangles, 12" x 18"

Making the Pillow

1. Cut a piece of freezer paper about 7" x 15". Place the freezer paper, shiny side down, over the wheat pattern on page 27 and use a pencil to trace the pattern. Make five tracings. Cut out the drawn leaves on the marked lines. ①

2. Cut five strips from the freezer paper, about ¼" x 10", to use as stems. You can cut these freehand for an organic look, or use a rotary cutter and ruler for a straight and precise graphic look. ②

3. Place the long skinny strips of freezer paper, shiny side down, on one of the muslin rectangles where you'd like the stems to be. In the pillow shown, the stems are placed about 3" apart. Position them, leaving some room at the top of the muslin rectangle; the strips can overhang the bottom edge.

When you're happy with the placement, use an iron to press them in place onto the muslin. ③

4. Place the leaves along the sides of the stems, shiny side down. Notice in the photograph on page 25 that they're not all aligned the same way; be as whimsical as you'd like. Secure them onto the muslin with the iron. ④

5. Following the manufacturer's instructions on the paint can, spray a light layer of paint all over the muslin. Let it sit for about a minute, then spray another light layer. Repeat until you get complete and even coverage on your muslin. There's no need to paint the backing rectangle. ⑤

Keep It Light

Use a light touch when applying the spray paint. If you apply the paint too heavily, it will seep through the fabric.

6. When the paint is completely dry (not tacky to touch), gently pull off the freezer-paper stencils from the muslin. ⑥

7. Place the two muslin rectangles right sides together and pin. Using a ¼"-wide seam allowance, sew around all four sides, leaving a 4" opening along the bottom edge. Turn right side out and press with an old terry-cloth towel over the painted side.

8. Stuff with fiberfill and hand stitch the opening closed.

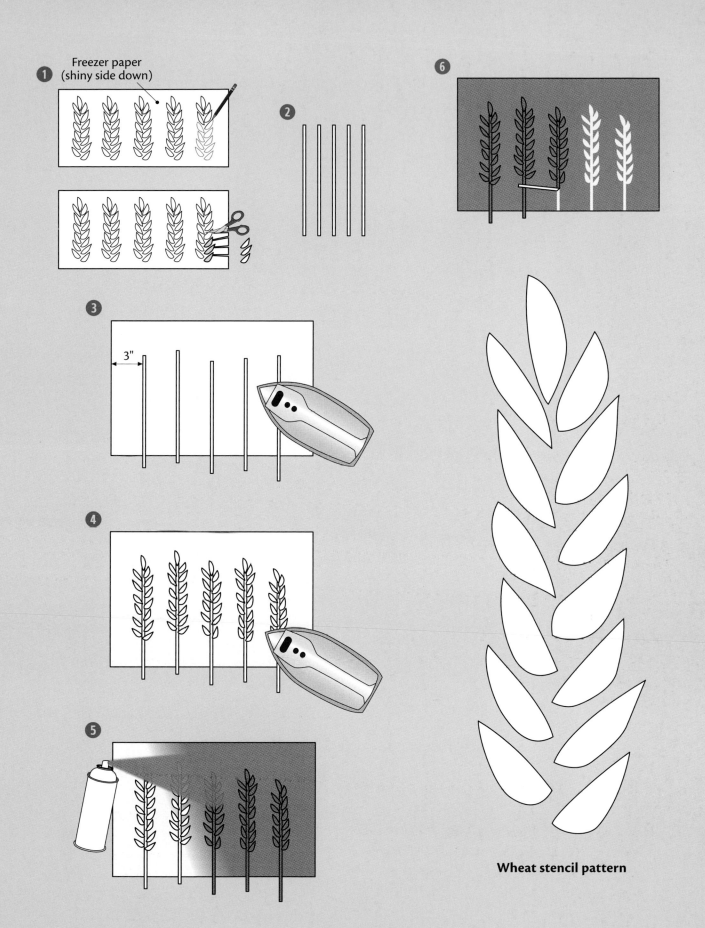

1 Freezer paper
(shiny side down)

2

3 3"

4

5

6

Wheat stencil pattern

Happy Mornings Embroidered Towels

Designed and made by Cynthia Tomaszewski

Doesn't everyone love chickens and roosters? Make these delightful kitchen towels for anyone on your gift list. Greeting the dawn with a favorite cup of coffee or tea along with these embroidered fowl will certainly give you something to crow about!

~Cynthia

Materials

2 purchased kitchen towels

1 skein each of 6-strand embroidery floss in red, green, gold, and black

2 black ¼"-diameter buttons

No. 2 pencil

Embroidery hoop

Embroidery needle

Stitching the Towels

1. Wash the towels and press.
2. Trace the embroidery designs on the towels, very lightly, using a No. 2 pencil.
3. Using two strands of the 6-strand embroidery floss, stem stitch the design, referring to "Embroidery Stitches" on page 107 for additional details.
4. Attach the black buttons for the eyes.

Button placement

Embroidery pattern

In Bloom Pillow

Designed and made by Sarah Bisel

Here's a great way to use some of those fabulous large-scale fabrics! You can choose your favorite fabric and use it as a focal point in one of these pillows. This is a fun and quick pillow to make for a friend or for yourself.

~Sarah

❀ **Finished pillow: 19½" x 19½"** ❀

Materials

Yardage is based on 42"-wide fabric.

1 yard of cotton or wool for pillow front and back
2½ yards of purchased piping
Scraps of felted wool for appliqués (or 10" x 30" piece)
Embroidery floss
20" x 20" pillow form
20" x 20" piece of lightweight fusible interfacing (optional)

Cutting

From the cotton or wool, cut:
1 square, 20" x 20"
2 rectangles, 14" x 20"

From the wool scraps, cut:
16 of template A
16 of template B
1 of template C

Individualize!

Make this pillow your own by choosing a style that fits you. You can choose lots of different colors for the petals, different prints for the front and back of the pillow, big bold prints, or calming hues. Make it your own. Note that the instructions include purchased piping to keep it simple and beginner-friendly.

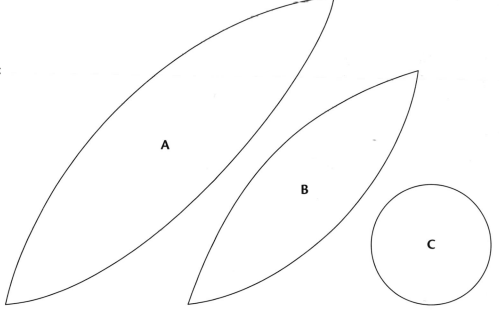

A

B

C

Appliquéing the Pillow Front

1. Find the center of the 20" square of fabric by folding it in first into quarters and then diagonally. Lightly press the folds to use as a placement guide. Adhere the A petals and flower center to the front of the pillow by pinning or lightly gluing. Fill in with additional A petals and then add an outer ring of B petals. ①

2. Using embroidery floss, hand appliqué the petals and flower center using a blanket stitch or whip-stitch. Refer to "Blanket Stitch" on page 106 for additional details. Or, if you choose, appliqué the petals using a blanket stitch on your sewing machine. Sarah uses her machine to do the blanket stitch, but she adjusts it to a larger size so that it looks more like the pillow has been hand stitched.

3. To add body and prevent the stitches from getting snagged when the pillow form is removed, add fusible interfacing to the wrong side of the pillow front, following the manufacturer's instructions.

Completing the Pillow

1. Hem one 20" side of each of the two pillow-back rectangles by double folding ¾" toward the wrong side and pressing. Topstitch along the folded edge. ②

2. Pin the piping to the right side of the pillow front, aligning the raw edges. Clip the piping as it rounds the corners so that it lies flat. ③

3. When the piping reaches the starting point, cut the end of the piping so it overlaps approximately 1". Remove 1" of stitches at the end of the piping to expose the cord within. Cut the ends of the cording so they touch without overlapping. Press under the fabric at the end of the piping to get a finished edge. ④

4. With right sides together, lay the pillow backs onto the pillow front, overlapping the back rectangles to fit the pillow front. Using a zipper foot, machine stitch as close as you can to the piping all around.

5. Turn the pillow cover right side out and insert the pillow form.

Make Do . . .

Not all pillow forms are made the same. So, let's say you make the pillow and the pillow form is too large or too small. Adjust the fit by adding some buttons and buttonholes in the back. It will look great, and it will fit even better. Use Velcro to hold the opening closed, and you can skip the buttonholes!

¾"
Fold

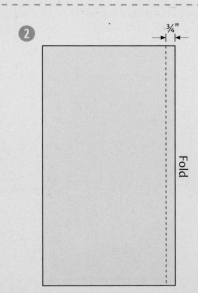

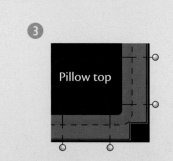

Pillow top

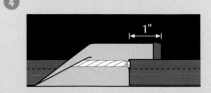

1"

Tic-Tac-Toe for Ewe Pillow

Designed and made by Cheryl Almgren Taylor

As enchanting as a real flock of sheep, this appliquéd pillow will be welcome in just about any setting. It's quick, easy, and useful. You'll enjoy making it as well as giving it. And whoever is on the receiving end will surely be pleased with this pastoral and plump interpretation of the classic tic-tac-toe.

~Cheryl

❀ **Finished pillow: 16" x 16"** ❀

Materials

Yardage is based on 42"-wide fabric.

⅞ yard of red print for pillow top and backing
¼ yard of black-and-white checked fabric for borders
1 fat quarter of black solid fabric for piping
1 fat quarter of green print for bias strips and leaves
Scraps of white, gray, and black prints for appliqués
⅓ yard of 20"-wide lightweight fusible web
Assorted matching threads for appliqué
16" x 16" pillow form

Cutting

From the red print, cut:
2 rectangles, 10½" x 16½"
1 square, 15" x 15"

From the black-and-white checked fabric, cut:
2 strips, 1½" x 16½"
2 strips, 1½" x 14½"

From the green print, cut:
4 bias strips, 1" x 12"

From the black solid, cut:
⅞" bias strips to total 70"

Making the Appliqué Block

1. Referring to "Fusible Appliqué" on page 108 and using the patterns on page 36, prepare six sheep appliqués and 32 leaf appliqués.

2. Locate the center of the red print 15" square by folding it in half lengthwise and widthwise. Draw a line 2" from the lengthwise center and 12" long; it should extend 6" above and below the midpoint. Repeat the process on the other side of the center, then widthwise. ①

3. Using matching thread, appliqué the green bias strips to the red print square along the lines by hand or machine, making a tic-tac-toe grid. Refer to "Easy Bias Strips" on page 36, or use your preferred method of making them.

4. Fuse the leaves and sheep appliqués in place, following the manufacturer's instructions.

5. Finish the raw edges on the appliqué pieces with a machine blanket stitch, zigzag, or satin stitch using matching thread.

6. Trim and square up the block to 14½" x 14½".

7. Sew the 1½" x 14½" border strips to opposite sides of the block and press the seam allowances toward the block. Sew the 1½" x 16½" border strips to the top and bottom of the block and press the seam allowances toward the block. ②

Adding the Piping

1. Refer to the "Easy Bias Strips" sidebar on page 36 for information on assembling bias strips. Sew together enough ⅞" strips to create a 70" length of bias fabric. Press the strip in half lengthwise, wrong sides together. ③

2. Placing the raw edges of the strip along the outside edge of the pillow top and leaving a 3" tail in front, baste the piping using a ¼" seam. At the corners, curve the piping as tightly as possible to go around them.

3. When you have sewn all four sides and are approximately 2½" from the beginning of the piping, fold over the left edge of the piping. Tuck the piping on the right inside the left piping. Sew in place. ④

Completing the Pillow

1. To make the pillow back, press under ¼" along one 16½" edge of each 10½" x 16½" red rectangle. Fold and press the edge again and stitch down the hem.

2. Place the backing rectangles right sides together with the pillow top, aligning the edges and overlapping the hemmed edges of the rectangles. Pin the pieces securely in place. Sew around the pillow directly on top of the piping stitching, using a ¼" seam allowance. ⑤

3. Turn the pillow right side out and insert a 16" pillow form through the opening in the back.

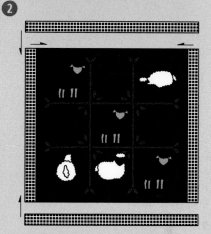

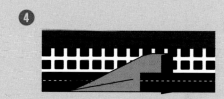

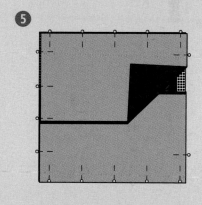

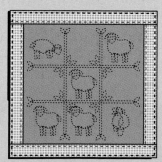

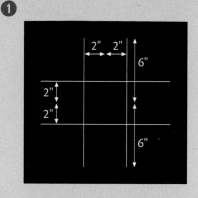

Patterns are reversed for fusible appliqué.

Sheep 1

Sheep 2

Leaf

Sheep 3

❋ EASY BIAS STRIPS

Cheryl uses the following method to make and apply bias strips.

1. Press a 1" x 12" bias strip in half lengthwise with wrong sides together.

2. Measuring from the folded edge, stitch the fabric together a hair wider than you want the bias strip to be. For the ¼"-wide bias strips used in this pillow, sew about ⁵/₁₆" from the fold.

3. Cut away the excess fabric along the raw edges so that you have about ¹/₁₆" of fabric remaining beyond the stitching line. ①

4. Mark the placement line on the background fabric. Align the raw edges of the bias strip along the line, making sure the bias strip extends below the line, not above it. Stitch the strip in place, sewing over the existing stitches. ②

5. Fold over and press the strip so the stitching is underneath. Cheryl sews the remaining edge by machine with invisible thread and a blind stitch, but you can also topstitch it or sew by hand. ③

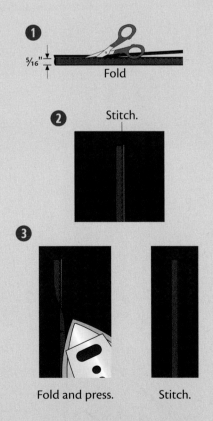

① ⁵/₁₆ " Fold

② Stitch.

③ Fold and press. Stitch.

It's My Birthday Pillow

Designed and made by Cindy Lammon

Unlike most adults, children are thrilled to share their age with you. One of my favorite things is to watch young children proudly displaying little fingers to announce how old they are. Make this adorable pillow so your little one can be reminded all year long how wonderful it is to be two, three, four, or more!

~Cindy

❀ **Finished size: 16" x 16"** ❀

Materials

Yardage is based on 42"-wide fabric.

1 fat quarter for pillow front
2 fat eighths for pillow front
Scraps for appliqués
¼ yard of fabric for binding
⅝ yard of fabric for pillow back
20" x 20" piece of batting
20" x 20" piece of muslin for lining*
½ yard of 12"-wide fusible web
16" x 16" pillow form

*This fabric will be inside the pillow and will not be visible.

Cutting

From the fat quarter, cut:
1 rectangle, 10¾" x 16"

From one fat eighth, cut:
1 strip, 1½" x 16"

From the second fat eighth, cut:
1 strip, 4¾" x 16"

From the pillow-back fabric, cut:
2 rectangles, 16" x 20"

From the binding fabric, cut:
2 strips, 3½" x 40"

Making the Pillow Top

1. Using a ¼" seam allowance, sew the 1½"-wide strip between the 4¾"-wide strip and the 10¾" x 16" rectangle along the 16" edges. Press the seam allowances toward the 1½"-wide strip. ①

2. Following the manufacturer's instructions for your fusible web, prepare the appliqués using the patterns on page 40.

3. Refer to the photo on page 37 and fuse the appliqué shapes in place. Stitch the edges with a buttonhole or zigzag stitch.

4. Quilting the top is optional, but it does make the pillow more stable. Layer the pillow top with the 20" x 20" muslin lining and batting. Quilt as desired. Cindy simply quilted in the ditch on either side of the narrow fabric strip. Stitch around the perimeter ¼" from the raw edges. Trim the batting and lining even with the pillow top.

Completing the Pillow

1. To create the pillow back, fold the two backing rectangles in half, wrong sides together, aligning the 16" edges; press.

2. Pin the pillow-back pieces to the wrong side of the pillow front, matching the raw edges. The folded edge of the back pieces will overlap in the center. Stitch around the perimeter ¼" from the raw edges. ②

3. Finish the edge of the pillow just like a quilt binding, except sew the binding to the pillow with a ½"-wide seam allowance. Refer to "Binding" on page 105. Fold the edge of the binding to the back of the pillow, mitering the corners. Hand or machine stitch.

4. Insert the pillow form.

Pillow Forms

You may notice that the pillow form is a bit larger than the pillow cover. This is intentional; it keeps your pillow looking fully stuffed and firm.

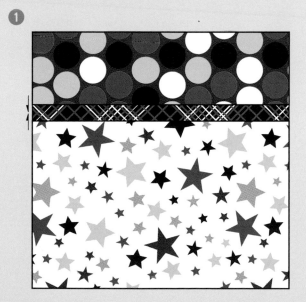

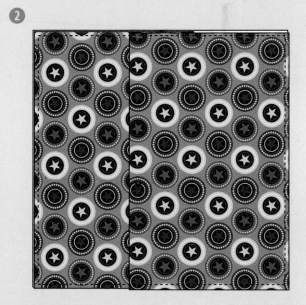

There's More Online!

To make patterns for the birthday numbers, you can either use your computer to print out a large number in a favorite font, or go to www.martingale-pub.com/extras/sewtheperfectgift to print out patterns for the numbers that Cindy used.

Cindy used Euphemia UCAS Bold font in 375 point size for her letters. As long as your letters are about 4⅛" tall, your pillow will look great. Just don't forget to reverse them before tracing them onto the fusible web.

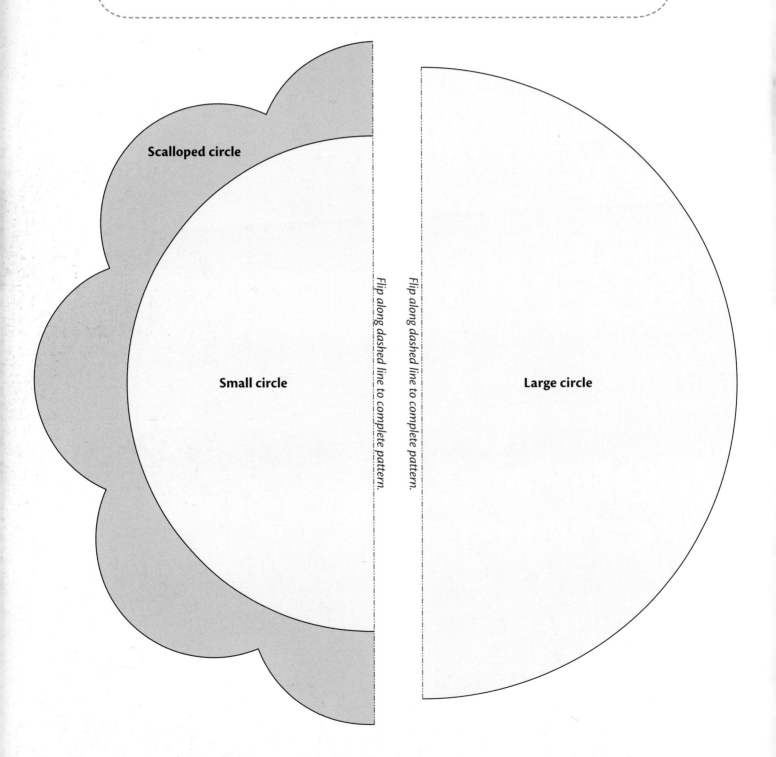

Scalloped circle

Small circle

Flip along dashed line to complete pattern.

Flip along dashed line to complete pattern.

Large circle

Knitter's Project Tote

Designed and made by Adrienne Smitke

Generously sized, this knitting bag is perfect for projects big and small and has plenty of pockets for needles and notions. If you want to make it for someone who's not a knitter, try personalizing the bag with an appliquéd monogram or initial instead. Either way, you'll have a perfect shopping-sized tote you can use every day or give as a gift. Fill it with knitting supplies or delicious goodies for an extra-special occasion.

~Adrienne

❀ **Finished size: 12" x 14" x 3"** ❀

Materials

Yardage is based on 42"-wide fabric.

1 yard of teal solid for outer bag, straps, and pockets

⅞ yard of lime green polka-dot fabric for bag lining and yarn-ball appliqué

½ yard of green-and-teal print for outer bag and pockets

2" x 8" piece of gray solid for knitting-needles appliqué

1⅓ yards of medium-weight 20"-wide fusible interfacing

¼ yard or scraps of 20"-wide fusible web

Cutting

From the teal solid, cut:

1 rectangle, 13" x 15", for outer back

1 rectangle, 8" x 15", for outer front

1 rectangle, 4" x 15", for outer side

1 rectangle, 4" x 13", for outer bottom

2 rectangles, 4" x 8", for side pockets

1 rectangle, 7" x 8", for pocket

2 strips, 6" x 24", for straps

From the green-and-teal print, cut:

1 rectangle, 6" x 15", for outer front

1 rectangle, 4" x 15", for outer side

2 rectangles, 4" x 8", for side pockets

1 rectangle, 7" x 8", for pocket

1 rectangle, 9" x 8", for pocket

From the lime green polka-dot fabric, cut:

2 rectangles, 13" x 15", for lining

2 rectangles, 4" x 15", for side lining

1 rectangle, 4" x 13", for bottom lining

2 rectangles, 8" x 13", for pocket lining

1 rectangle, 5" x 8", for pocket

From the interfacing, cut:

1 rectangle, 13" x 15", for outer back

1 rectangle, 8" x 15", for outer front

1 rectangle, 6" x 15", for outer front

2 rectangles, 4" x 15", for outer sides

1 rectangle, 4" x 13", for outer bottom

2 rectangles, 4" x 8", for outer side pockets

Making the Outer Bag

Use a ½" seam allowance throughout unless otherwise directed.

1. Fuse the rectangles of interfacing for the outer bag to the *wrong* sides of the corresponding fabric outer-bag pieces, including the teal solid 8" x 15", 13" x 15", 4" x 15", and 4" x 13" rectangles, and the green-and-teal print 6" x 15" and 4" x 15" rectangles. *Do not fuse the interfacing to the side pocket pieces yet.*

2. Using the appliqué patterns on page 46 and referring to "Fusible Appliqué" on page 108, prepare the appliqués. Use the lime green polka-dot fabric for the yarn ball and the gray solid for the knitting needles.

3. Fuse the knitting needles and yarn ball to the teal solid 8" x 15" rectangle as shown. Blanket stitch around the edges and topstitch the yarn details with matching thread. ①

4. With right sides together, sew the appliquéd rectangle to the green-and-teal print 6" x 15" rectangle. Press the seam allowance open. Topstitch ⅛" away on both sides of the seam and then again ¼" from the first set of stitching lines. ②

5. To make the side pockets, fuse a 4" x 8" interfacing rectangle to the wrong side of one teal solid 4" x 8" rectangle and one green-and-teal print 4" x 8" rectangle. Pair each interfaced rectangle with a 4" x 8" rectangle of the opposite-colored fabric. Sew the pocket pieces right sides together, across the top edge. Turn right side out and topstitch ⅛" from the top seam and then again ¼" from the first stitching line. ③

6. Pin a matching side pocket to each 4" x 15" outer-side piece, aligning the bottom raw edges. Sew a side unit to each side of the appliquéd panel. Stop stitching ½" before the bottom of the unit, backstitching at the beginning and end of the seam. Sew the teal solid 13" x 15" rectangle to the end of this unit as shown, stopping ½" from the bottom and backstitching. Press all seam allowances open. ④

7. With right sides together, sew the ends of the unit to create a tube, again stopping ½" before the bottom of the unit and backstitching at the beginning and end. Press the seam allowance open. ⑤

8. With right sides together, pin the teal solid 4" x 13" rectangle to the bottom of the tube. Fold up the bottom corners of the tube at a 90° angle so that it sits flat against the bag bottom. ⑥

9. Starting in the middle of one of the long sides, stitch the tube to the bottom of the bag. When you reach each corner, keep your machine needle down and

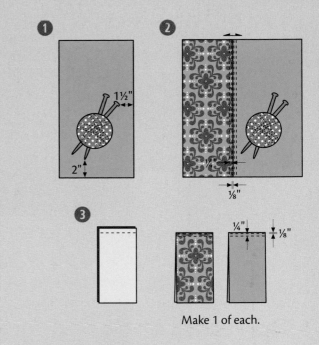

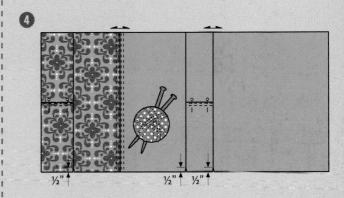

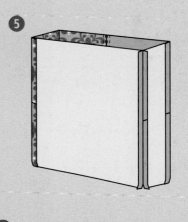

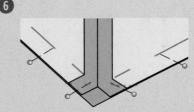

Make 1 of each.

pivot to take a couple stitches across the corner at a 45° angle; then backstitch to tack the corner securely in place. Stitch forward and pivot to continue stitching all the way around. Trim the excess fabric at the corners, making sure not to cut too close to the seam. Then turn the outer bag right side out. ⑦

Making the Bag Lining

1. To make the inside pockets, sew a lime green polka-dot 5" x 8" rectangle and a green-and-teal print 9" x 8" rectangle, right sides together, along the 8" edges. Press the seam allowance open. Repeat with a green-and-teal 7" x 8" rectangle and a teal solid 7" x 8" rectangle.

2. Pair each pocket with a lime polka-dot 8" x13" rectangle, right sides together. Sew together along the 13" edge. Turn the pockets right side out and

topstitch ⅛" from the seam and then again ¼" from that stitching line. ⑧

3. Pin each pocket to a 13" x 15" lime polka-dot rectangle, aligning the bottom raw edges. Stitch each pocket to the lining by topstitching ⅛" on each side of the seam between the different-colored pockets and then again ¼" from the first set of stitching lines. ⑨

4. To assemble the lining, sew the pocket sections from step 3 together with the lime polka-dot 4" x 15" rectangles to make a tube as you did when making the outer bag. For the lining, however, leave a 6" opening on one side seam and backstitch on either end of the opening. ⑩

5. Sew the 4" x 13" lime polka-dot bottom lining to the tube from step 4, following steps 8 and 9 of "Making the Outer Bag" on page 43. Do not turn the lining right side out.

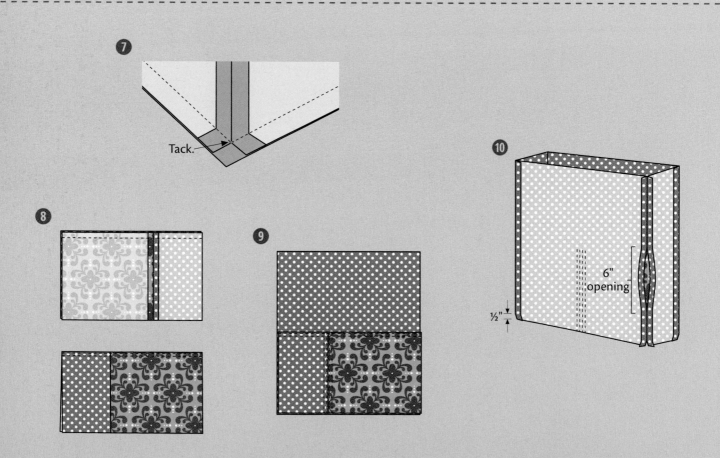

Tack.

6" opening

½"

Making the Straps and Assembling the Bag

1. Fold a teal solid 6" x 24" strip in half *lengthwise*, wrong sides together. Press to create a crease down the center of the strip. Open the strip to reveal the crease. Fold the raw edges of the strip into the center crease you just made; press. Fold the strip in half on the crease, enclosing the raw edges of the strip in the center of the strap. Topstitch both sides a scant ⅛" from the edge and down the center of the strap. Make two straps. ⑪

2. Pin the strap to the front of the outer bag, 1½" from each edge. Repeat for the second strap on the back of the bag. Then, with right sides together, slip the outer bag inside the bag lining. ⑫

3. Align the top raw edges, matching the side seams, and pin or clip them together. Stitch all the way around the top edge. Turn the bag right side out by pulling the entire bag through the opening you left in the side of the lining. Whipstitch the opening closed with a matching thread. ⑬

> ## Shortcut
>
> If you're in a hurry to finish, you can close the opening in the lining by machine.

4. Push the lining inside the outer bag and iron the bag, paying extra attention to the top seam of the bag, so that the seam allowance is nice and flat and the lining doesn't show on the outside. Topstitch ⅜" from the edge around the top of the bag.

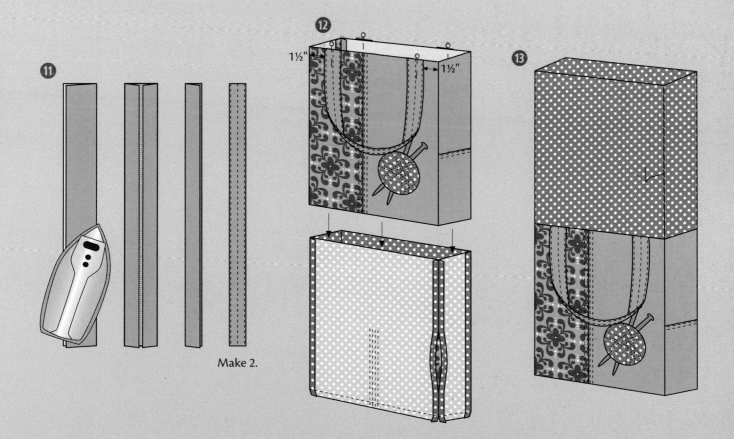

Make 2.

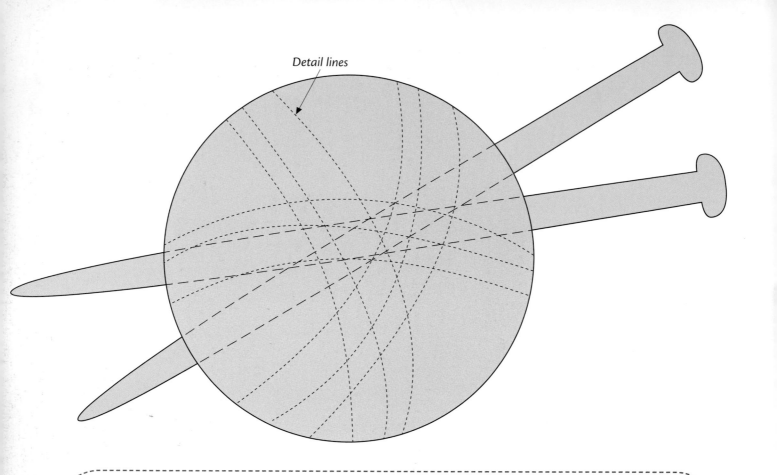

Detail lines

There's More Online!

If you have several friends who love knitting and you don't want to make the same gift for each of them, you'll find free patterns for this handy Knitter's Trio online at www.martingale-pub.com/extras/sewtheperfectgift.

You can easily customize the double-pointed needle roll, circular needle hanger, and ditty bag to reflect each recipient's favorite colors. This project group is easy to complete and requires just a little fabric, so in an afternoon or two you can whip up a chic gift.

Green Thumb Gardener's Apron

Designed and made by Cassie Barden

This quick, pretty apron is the perfect gift for the gardener in your life—even if that person is you! I used vinyl-coated cottons in gorgeous prints for this version, but you can use oilcloth as well (though it will add a bit more bulk). Either choice sheds dirt and water with ease. A variety of pockets will hold seeds and shears, and the added canvas protects against pointy garden tools. This apron would work equally well for art supplies or workshop tools, so adjust the size and number of pockets to suit.

~Cassie

❀ **Finished apron: 12" x 20"** ❀

Materials

Yardage is based on 54"-wide fabric. Cassie used vinyl-coated cotton for the large- and small-scale prints.

⅓ yard large-scale floral print for apron and apron
     tie ends
¼ yard small-scale print for apron pocket
½ yard off-white canvas for pockets and apron backing
2½ yards of 1½"-wide cotton webbing for apron tie
Chalk pencil

Cutting

From the large-scale floral print, cut:

1 rectangle, 10" x 21"

From the small-scale print, cut:

1 rectangle, 6" x 21"

From the canvas, cut:

1 rectangle, 13" x 21"
1 rectangle, 9" x 21"
1 strip, 4" x 21"

Making the Apron

Use a ½" seam allowance unless otherwise specified.

1. With right sides together, stitch the 9" x 21" canvas rectangle to the 6" x 21" rectangle along the 21" edge. Using a cool iron and avoiding too much direct contact with the laminate, press the seam allowance toward the laminate.

2. Fold the finished unit in half lengthwise and press the top fold. Topstitch the print through all layers about ⅛" from the seam, edge to edge, to make the pocket unit. ①

3. Sew the 4" x 21" canvas strip along the bottom edge of the 10" x 21" floral-print rectangle and press the seam allowance toward the print.

4. Mark stitching lines onto the front of the pocket unit as shown using a chalk pencil. Layer the pocket unit onto the floral rectangle, pin in the seam allowances, and stitch through all layers along the marked lines, backstitching at the top edge of the pocket for reinforcement. ②

5. Layer the remaining 13" x 21" canvas rectangle over this finished unit, right sides together. Stitch around the perimeter, leaving 10" unsewn in the center of the top edge. Trim the corners and turn the apron inside out. Fold the seam allowances toward

the inside along the opening and press all the edges with a cool iron. ③

6. Topstitch around the entire perimeter, including the opening from step 5.

7. Center the cotton-webbing tie along the top edge of the apron, with the tie underneath, and pin. Stitch the tie down as shown, sewing over the topstitching done in step 6. ④

8. Try on the apron and trim the webbing if desired. Cassie left it long to tie in a bow. To keep the tie ends from fraying and to add a nice finishing touch, cut two rectangles, 1⅝" x 2¼", from the floral print. Fold a rectangle over a tie end. Using a small zigzag stitch, stitch around the rectangle as shown. Repeat for the other tie end. ⑤

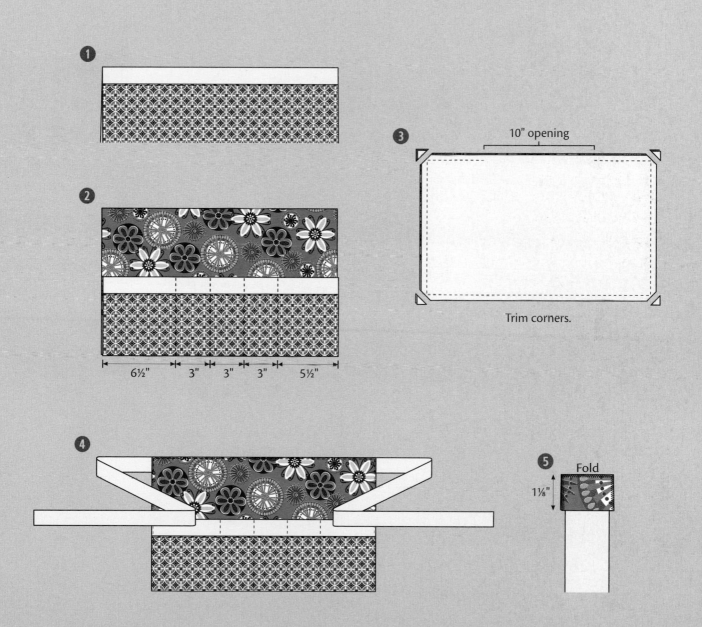

6½"   3"   3"   3"   5½"

10" opening

Trim corners.

Fold

1⅛"

Curling-Iron Cozy

Designed and made by Barbara Groves and Mary Jacobson
of Me and My Sister Designs

This easy project is perfect for a friend who travels. The Curling-Iron Cozy does double duty to store a curling iron at home! With the cozy's thermal batting, you'll no longer need to set your warm curling iron out to cool near the bathroom sink. Just place it in this handy case and keep the clutter off the bathroom countertop.

~ Barbara & Mary

❀ **Finished size: 5¾" x 14½"** ❀

Materials

1 fat quarter for outside of case
1 fat quarter for inside of case
12" x 15" piece of thermal batting*
2 large coordinating buttons
Embroidery floss for tying buttons
Basting spray

Use a heat-resistant batting, such as Insul-Bright from the Warm Company.

Cutting

From *each* of the fat quarters, cut:
1 rectangle, 12" x 15"

Assembling the Cozy

1. Using the basting spray, generously spray one side of the 12" x 15" thermal batting piece. Be sure to do this outside in a well-ventilated area. Spraying the batting eliminates slipping and allows you to quilt the pieces later without pinning or basting.

2. Center and place the sticky side of the thermal-batting piece onto the *wrong* side of the rectangle for the outside of the cozy. Press together firmly with your hands or lightly press with a cool iron.

3. Quilt this layered rectangle (right side up) as desired. Barbara and Mary stitched simple straight lines that crisscross the rectangle. Start by sewing diagonally from corner to corner. Stitch parallel lines outward at 1" intervals in both directions. Repeat the process by stitching diagonally from the opposite two corners. ①

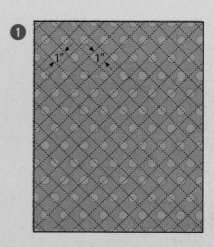

4. Some stretching may occur during quilting, so trim the quilted rectangle to measure 12" x 15".

5. With *right* sides together, layer the fabric rectangle for the inside of the cozy onto the quilted rectangle. (The batting will be on the bottom.) Using a ¼" seam allowance, stitch around all four sides, leaving a 5" opening along one of the short sides for turning. Backstitch at both ends. ②

6. Trim all excess batting away from the seam allowances and clip corners. Gently turn the cozy right side out. Turn the raw edges at the opening to the inside, press flat, and pin in place.

7. Topstitch ¼" from the edges around the entire rectangle.

8. With the inside of the cozy facing up, fold the rectangle in half lengthwise so that the rectangle now measures 5¾" x 14½" and the opening that you just sewed closed is at the bottom. The outside of the cozy is now showing. ③

9. Measure 4½" down from the top of the cozy and mark with a pin. Begin sewing at this point, stitching the remainder of the open side and across the bottom, between the outer edge and the previous topstitching line. Backstitch at both ends. ④

10. Fold down one of the top flaps to the front of the cozy and attach the buttons with embroidery floss. ⑤

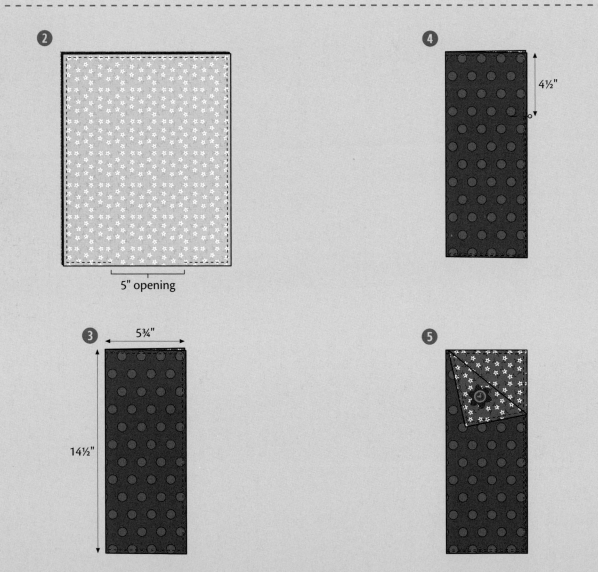

❷

5" opening

❹

4½"

❸

5¾"

14½"

❺

Heartfelt Journal

Designed and made by Cheryl Lynch

Here's a joyful wool journal cover designed for a composition notebook. Stitching this one out of felted wool makes it a fast project and fun to sew. Every time it's written in, the recipient will think of you, and when the notebook is full, the cover can be transferred onto a new one.

~Cheryl

Materials

See page 107 for instructions on felting wool.

10" x 21" piece of light green felted wool for journal cover

6" square of magenta felted wool for medium heart, small hearts, and pen pocket

4" x 5" piece of black-and-white checked felted wool for large heart

2½" x 6½" piece of blue felted wool for large circles

1½" x 4½" piece of green checked felted wool for small circles

¾ yard of ½"-wide pink rickrack

5 buttons, ⅜" diameter

Wool-blend embroidery thread or size 5 pearl cotton in light blue and magenta

7½" x 9¾" composition notebook

Freezer paper

Chenille needle, size 22

Preparing the Wool Appliqués

Felted wool does not have a right side or a wrong side, so either side can be used.

1. Trace the appliqué-pattern pieces shown on page 56 onto the dull paper side of the freezer paper using a pencil. Cut out the number of pieces indicated on the pattern pieces. Group together pieces that will be cut from the same piece of wool for the most efficient cutting. ①

2. Iron the freezer paper onto the wool, using a hot, dry iron, with the waxy side down.

3. Cut out the appliqué pieces on the drawn lines and carefully remove the freezer paper.

Appliquéing the Cover

1. Referring to "Blanket Stitch" on page 106, stitch the small circles to the large circles with the magenta thread. Stitch the medium heart to the large heart with the light blue thread.

2. To make sure that the appliqué design is centered on the journal cover, lay the wool for the cover flat on a table. Measure 3" from each side. Fold toward the middle to form a flap and pin in place. (Do a quick check to make sure this fits the notebook.) ②

3. Fold the cover in half and lay out the wool appliqué pieces for the design on the front as shown and generously pin in place. Unpin the flaps to facilitate stitching. ③

4. Cut three pieces of rickrack for the stems: cut one piece 4" long and two pieces 3" long.

5. Stack the three rickrack stems and then tack them to the cover, using a sewing machine if possible, underneath the large heart appliqué. Pin them in place as shown so that they end underneath the large circle appliqués. Trim if necessary. ④

6. Blanket stitch the circles with the light blue thread, and the heart with the magenta thread to the wool journal cover.

7. Stitch the rickrack stems in place using the magenta thread and French knots, referring to "Embroidery Stitches" on page 107 if needed. ⑤

8. Blanket-stitch across the top of the pen pocket using the light blue thread. Without cutting the thread, position the pocket on the inside front cover and blanket-stitch around the sides and bottom. ⑥

9. Pin the flaps back in place. Thread the needle with approximately 2 yards of light blue thread and use it to blanket stitch across the entire top edge. Repeat for the bottom edge. ⑦

10. Attach the buttons to the circle flowers with the magenta thread.

Completing the Cover

1. Cut a 12" length of rickrack and place it between two small hearts. Using the light blue thread, secure the rickrack by taking a few stitches through all the layers, hiding the knot inside. Attach a button to each side of the heart and then blanket stitch the hearts together. ⑧

2. Find the center of the top edge of the journal cover and sew the rickrack to the inside perpendicular to the top edge. ⑨

3. To fit the cover onto the notebook, first place the front cover into the front flap. Fold the back cover so that it is almost touching the front cover. Then slide the back cover of the notebook into the back flap.

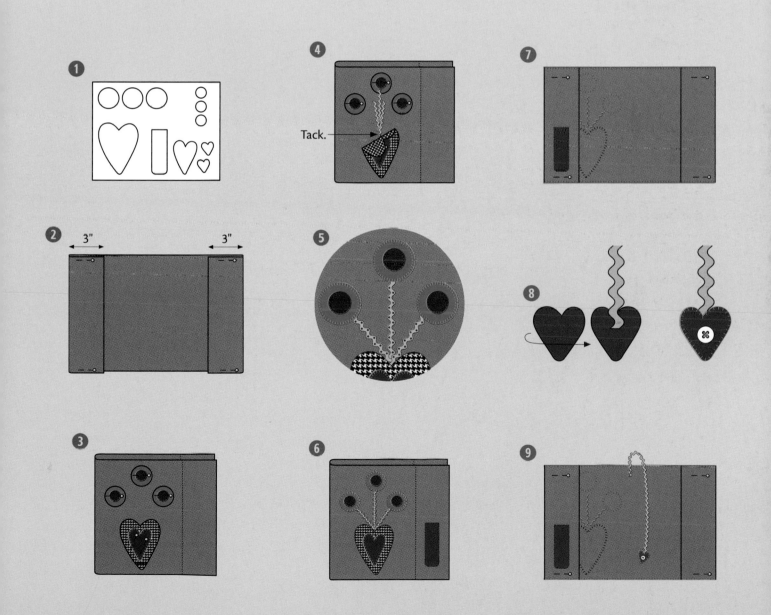

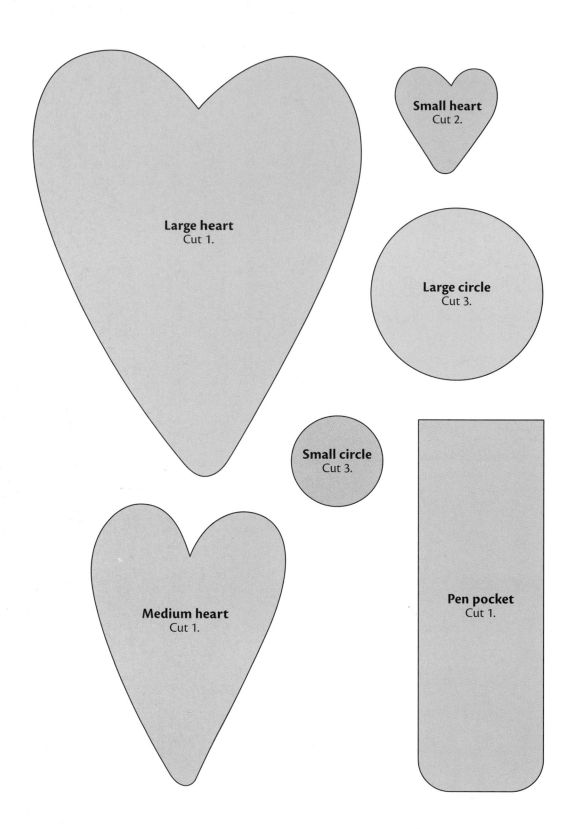

Large heart
Cut 1.

Small heart
Cut 2.

Large circle
Cut 3.

Small circle
Cut 3.

Medium heart
Cut 1.

Pen pocket
Cut 1.

Posy Pincushion
Designed and made by Linda Lum DeBono

This quick-and-easy design is perfect to make for all your friends who love to quilt and sew. Who wouldn't want this adorable bouquet adorning her sewing station? While you're at it, go ahead and make one for yourself.

~Linda

❀ **Finished size: 3½" x 5" x 2½"** ❀

Materials

See page 107 for instructions on felting wool.

9" x 12" piece of light pink felted wool for flower petals

7" x 9" piece of white felted wool for top and bottom of pincushion

7" x 9" piece of light green felted wool for pincushion sides

6" x 6" square of moss green felted wool for leaves

3" x 6" piece of dark pink felted wool for flower centers

Embroidery floss in white and colors to match wool and beads

Embroidery needle

30–36 beads for flower centers

16-ounce bag of polyester fiberfill

Wave-edge fabric shears for cutting leaves (optional)

Cutting

The patterns for the pincushion are on page 59.

From the light pink felted wool, cut:

15 petals

From the dark pink felted wool, cut:

3 circles

From the white felted wool, cut:

2 ovals

From the light green felted wool, cut:

2 rectangles, 2½" x 7¼"

From the moss green felted wool, cut:

5 leaves using the leaf pattern on page 59, or use wave-edge fabric shears to cut free-form leaves.

Assembling the Flower

1. Thread an embroidery needle with pink floss and knot the end. Starting with one pink petal, place point A on top of point B and stitch together. Do not cut the thread. Sew the tips of a second petal in the same manner, joining it to the first petal. Continue to sew the tips of each petal in the same manner while joining one petal to the next at the same time to form a chain of petals. Pull tight together after adding each petal. When five petals are sewn together, form a circle with the petals and join the last petal to the first petal. ①

2. Layer the flower center on top of the gathered petals and sew through all of the layers. Randomly place beads as you are stitching through the center.

3. Repeat steps 1 and 2 to make two more flowers.

4. Arrange the leaves and flowers as you like on the white oval and stitch to the oval. This will become the top of the pincushion. ②

Assembling the Pincushion

1. Layer the green rectangles, and using a ¼" seam allowance, sew along both short ends by machine as shown to make the pincushion sides. ③

2. Fold the plain white oval in half lengthwise and crease lightly. Pin one white oval to the edge of the pincushion side, aligning the crease with the side seams of the rectangles. Using two strands of white embroidery floss, hand sew the pieces together using a blanket stitch. Refer to "Blanket Stitch" on page 106 for details if needed. ④

3. Attach the adorned white oval in the same manner to the other side of the green rectangles for the top of the pincushion, but stop stitching 2" from the starting point to leave an opening for stuffing. *Do not cut the floss.*

Topsy-Turvy Stitching

Try turning the pincushion upside down when you're pinning and blanket stitching around the top. This helps to keep the flower petals out of the way.

4. Firmly stuff the pincushion with polyester fiberfill and then continue sewing the blanket stitch to close the opening.

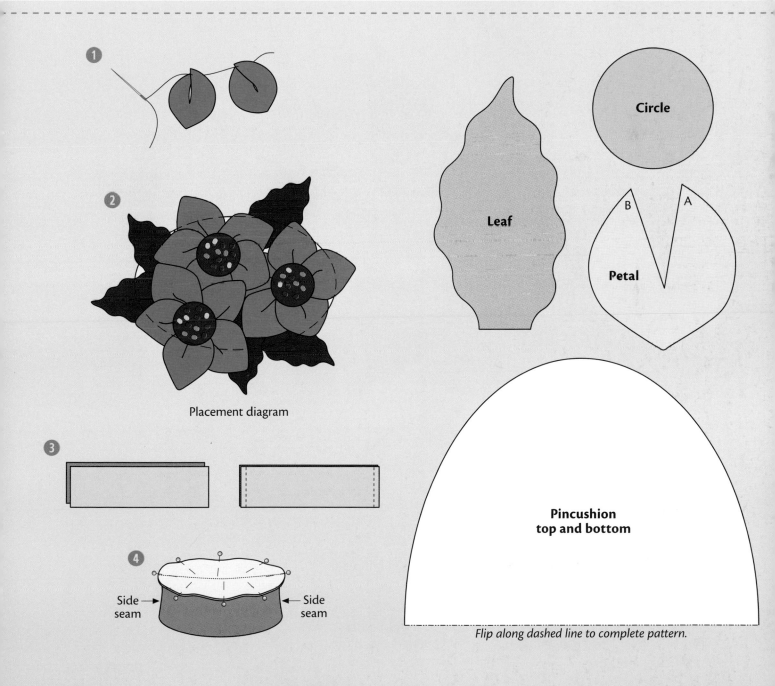

Placement diagram

Circle

Leaf

B   A

Petal

Pincushion
top and bottom

Flip along dashed line to complete pattern.

Side seam   Side seam

Swingy Shoulder Bag

Designed and made by Kim Diehl

Here's an ideal bag for any fashionable, on-the-go woman. It's the perfect size for every day with interior pockets to keep items organized. Make the Swingy Shoulder Bag or the extra-swingy variation that has longer handles designed to be worn across the body. One thing is certain, with all the marvelous fabrics in shops today, you'll have a ball choosing prints to match the recipient's style!

~Kim

❀ **Finished size: 12" x 23" x 3" (including handle)** ❀

Materials

Yardage is based on 42"-wide fabric.

¾ yard of print for outer bag*

¾ yard of coordinating print for lining*

¾ yard of muslin for inner lining*

36" length of freezer paper

Acrylic ruler

Water-soluble marker

All-purpose thread in a color to complement the
    outer bag for topstitching

For the Extra-Swingy Shoulder Bag shown at right, you'll need 1 yard of each fabric.

Preparing the Pattern Pieces

1. Use a pencil and acrylic ruler to trace pattern pieces 1–3 on pages 65–67. Begin with pattern piece 1 and start at the bottom of the freezer paper. Overlap each new pattern piece with the previously traced piece along the dashed lines.

2. Trace the bag bottom onto the unused area of the freezer paper.

3. Cut out each pattern piece exactly on the drawn lines (the ¼" seam allowance is included in the patterns). Transfer the "center" and "leave open" markings onto the pattern pieces. To achieve a crisp, straight edge along each pattern piece, Kim used a rotary cutter and acrylic ruler for the straight portion of the patterns and scissors for the curves.

❀ EXTRA-SWINGY SHOULDER BAG

**Finished size: 12" x 32" x 3"
(including handle)**

Trace pattern pieces 1–4 onto freezer paper as instructed in "Preparing the Pattern Pieces" at left. Follow the remaining project instructions to make this cross-body version of the Swingy Shoulder Bag.

Cutting

1. Lay out the fabric for the outer bag as it comes off the bolt, with the existing center fold and the selvage edges together. Fold the selvage edges over toward the original center fold to make four layers of fabric measuring 8" in width, leaving a 5" margin between the selvage edges and the original fold. Press the newly formed double fold flat. ①

2. Lay the bag pattern piece onto the four-layered side of fabric, placing the center pattern edge flush with the pressed fold as indicated. Press the freezer paper in place and pin through the pattern piece and fabric layers as shown to keep the layers from shifting. Cut out the fabric exactly along the pattern edges; *do not* cut through the fabric folds at the bag center. Use a water-soluble marker to transfer the "leave open" markings onto the handle. Remove the pattern and unfold the fabric to yield two bag pieces. ②

3. Repeat steps 1 and 2 with the lining and muslin fabrics, omitting the "leave open" markings.

4. To cut a pocket piece for the inside of the bag, use the remaining outer-bag print along the original single fold to cut a 4½" x 16" rectangle; you will be cutting through two layers of fabric, leaving the fold intact. The cut rectangle will have a lengthwise center fold, with the right sides of the print facing outward. (If unfolded, it will measure 9" x 16".)

5. Cut a bag bottom from the remainder of each of the three fabrics (outer bag, lining, muslin) along the original single fold as shown. Align the straight edge of the pattern piece with the folded fabric edge. Press in place and pin the fabric layers. Cut out the bottom piece exactly along the pattern edge; *do not* cut through the fabric fold. Remove the pattern and unfold the fabric to yield the bag-bottom pieces. ③

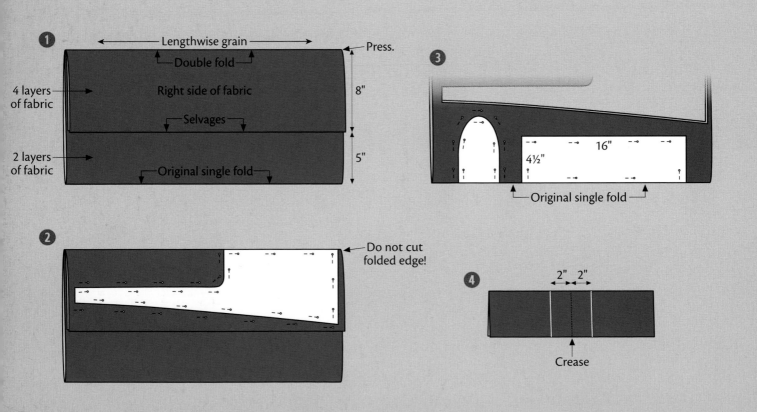

① Lengthwise grain — Press.
Double fold
4 layers of fabric — Right side of fabric — 8"
Selvages
2 layers of fabric — Original single fold — 5"

② Do not cut folded edge!

③ 16" — 4½" — Original single fold

④ 2" 2" — Crease

Sewing the Bag

All seam allowances are ¼" unless otherwise noted.

1. Fold the 4½" x 16" pocket piece in half to find the center and use a hot, dry iron to press a crease. Use a water-soluble marker and acrylic ruler to draw a vertical line 2" from each side of the center crease. ④

2. Center and layer the prepared pocket rectangle onto the right side of one bag lining piece, with the fold positioned upward and the bottom raw edges even with the bottom raw edge of the lining piece. Pin securely in place. From the wrong side of the lining, stay stitch these pieces together along the lining edge using a scant ⅛" seam allowance. Trim away the excess pocket fabric, using the lining piece as a guide. ⑤

3. Beginning at the bottom raw edge, stitch upward along one of the drawn lines on the pocket to divide it into sections and attach it to the lining. When you are approximately ½" from the top fold of the pocket, stop stitching with your needle down, pivot, and stitch at an angle outward. Then stitch across the fabric near the top of the fold and back down to the center stitched line to form a triangle. Stitch along the triangle a second time for added strength, and then continue stitching back to the bottom raw edge of the lining. Repeat with the second drawn line. ⑥

4. With *wrong* sides together (you should be able to see the "pretty" side of the lining print), layer and pin one lining and muslin bag piece together. Use a scant ⅛" seam allowance to stay stitch around the entire perimeter of the pieces to form a double lining. Repeat with the second lining and muslin bag pieces. In the same manner, stay stitch the lining and muslin bottom pieces with wrong sides together. ⑦

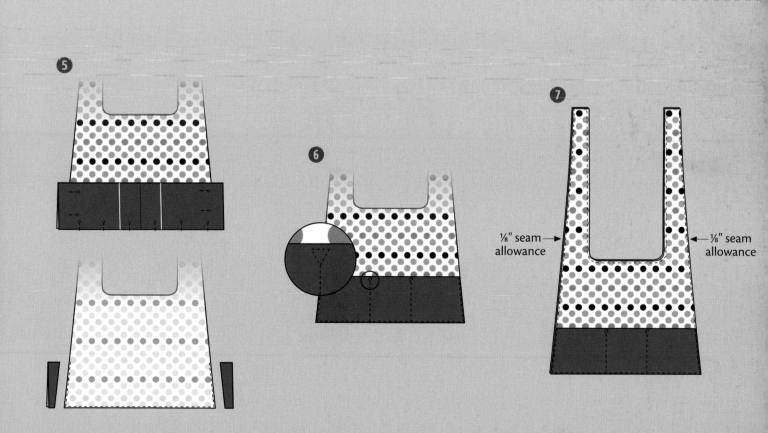

⅛" seam allowance ⅛" seam allowance

5. Layer the two stay-stitched lining pieces with right sides together. Pin securely in place along the long outer edges. Using a ¼" seam allowance, stitch through the layers along the long outer edges *only*, proceeding all the way to the top of the handle. Press the seam allowances open. In the same manner, sew the outer-bag pieces together, disregarding the "leave open" markings at this time. ⑧

6. With right sides together, align the center point on each end of the bag-bottom lining with the side seams of the bag-lining unit. Pin securely in place, working out from each rounded end to the center point on each side. Stitch the pinned pieces together twice, placing the second round of stitches exactly over the first sewn seam line to reinforce the bag bottom. Press the seam allowances away from the bag bottom. ⑨

7. Repeat step 6 with the outer-bag and bag-bottom pieces. Turn the outer bag right side out.

8. With the muslin side of the bag-lining unit facing outward, insert the outer bag into the lining so that the lining print and outer-bag prints are positioned with right sides together. Line up the side seams and pin the outer-bag and lining pieces together along the lower shoulder-strap edges and bag opening until you reach the "leave open" markings.

9. Beginning and ending with a locking or backstitch, sew the pinned edges together, starting and stopping at the marked positions on the handle (this portion of the handle will be stitched together after the bag has been turned right side out).

10. Turn the bag right side out through one of the strap openings, carefully using a wooden dowel or the blunt end of a knitting needle if needed. The lining should now rest inside the bag.

11. With right sides together, stitch the loose outer-strap ends together to join the bag handle into one continuous piece. Press the seam allowance open. In the same manner, stitch and press the loose lining-strap ends.

12. Press the bag opening and sewn portion of the straps flat along the seamed outer edges. Turn the unsewn length of the outer-strap edges under ¼" and press in place; repeat with the lining strap. Align the pressed layers of the lining and outer-strap edges where they are unstitched and pin them securely through all layers to prevent shifting. Continue pinning the layers together along the remaining outer edges of the strap and bag opening. Topstitch the edge of the pinned layers along each side of the strap and bag opening, sewing just inside the edges. Remove the pins and press the bag well to remove any wrinkles. ⑩

Muslin side out

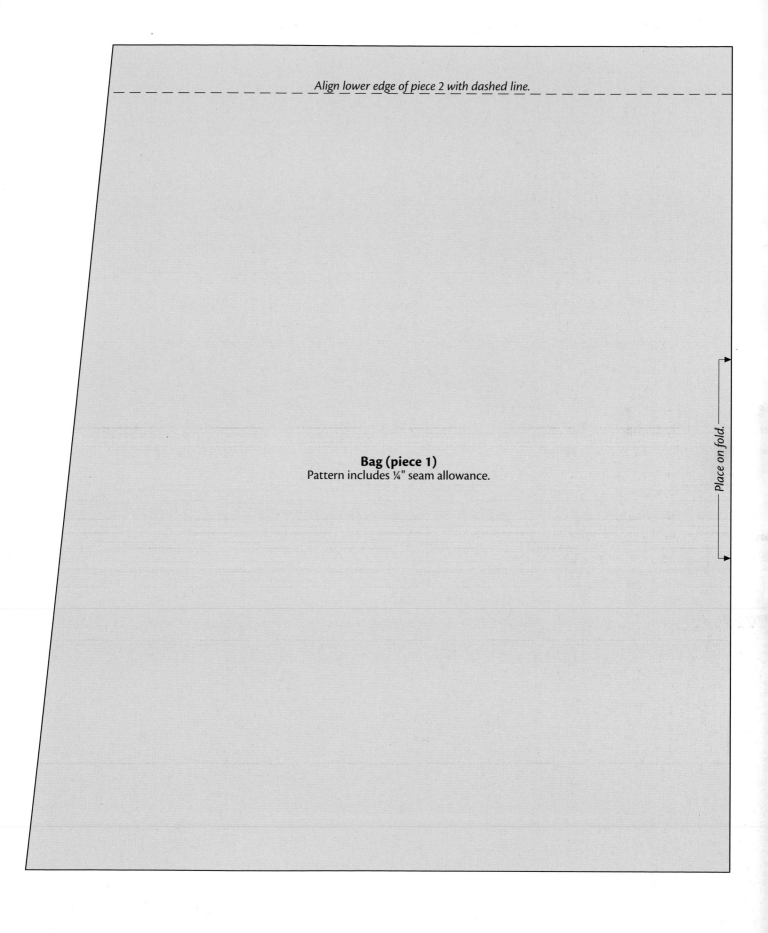

Align lower edge of piece 2 with dashed line.

Bag (piece 1)
Pattern includes ¼" seam allowance.

Place on fold.

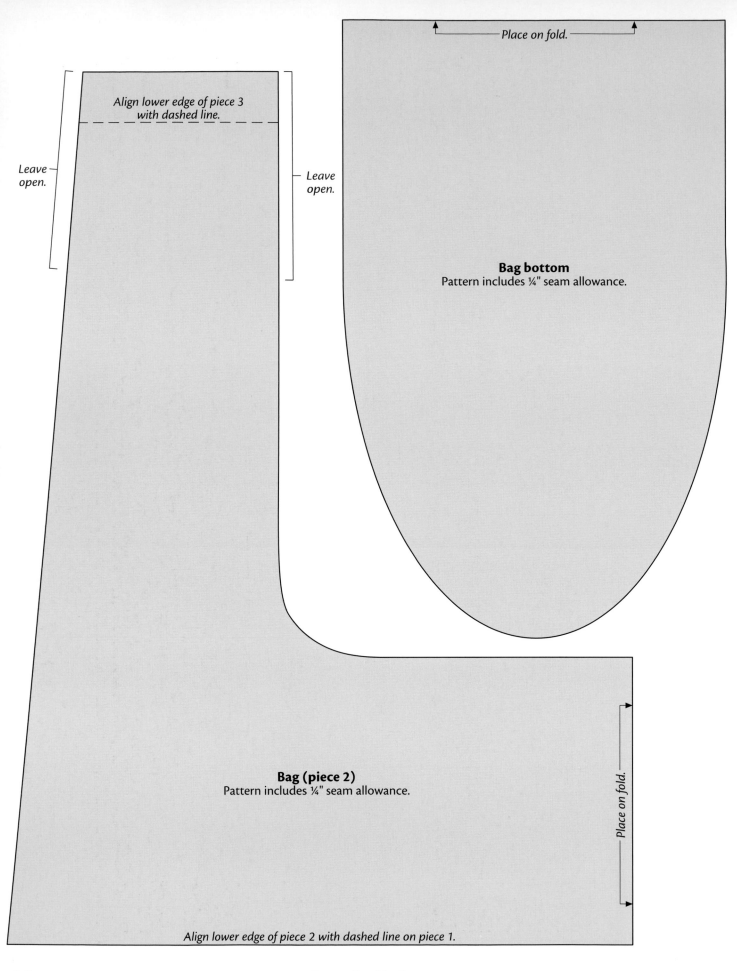

Place on fold.

Bag bottom
Pattern includes ¼" seam allowance.

Align lower edge of piece 3 with dashed line.

Leave open.

Leave open.

Place on fold.

Bag (piece 2)
Pattern includes ¼" seam allowance.

Align lower edge of piece 2 with dashed line on piece 1.

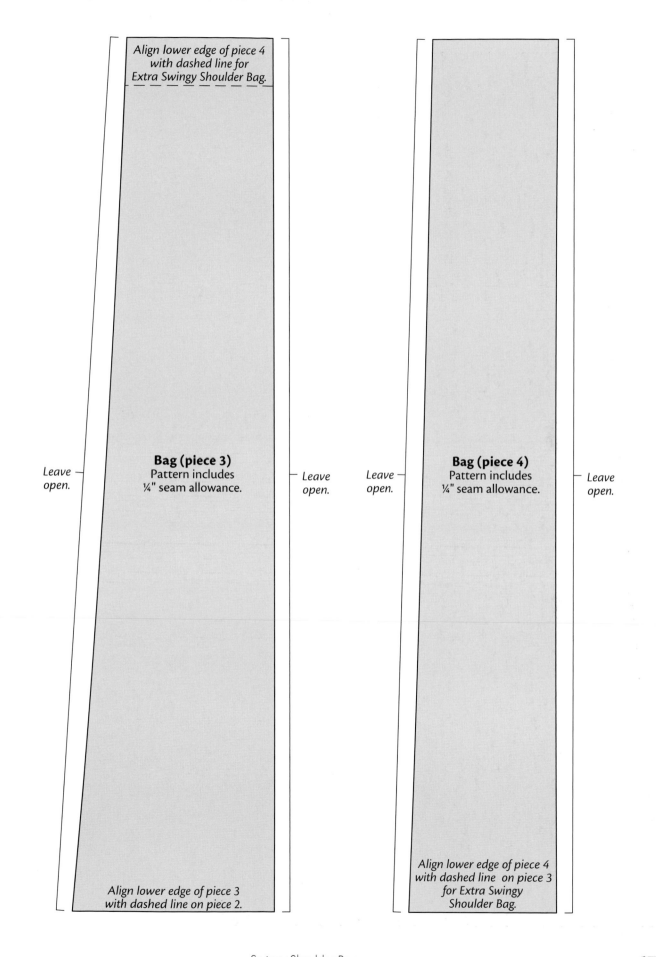

Align lower edge of piece 4 with dashed line for Extra Swingy Shoulder Bag.

Bag (piece 3)
Pattern includes
¼" seam allowance.

Leave open.

Leave open.

Align lower edge of piece 3 with dashed line on piece 2.

Bag (piece 4)
Pattern includes
¼" seam allowance.

Leave open.

Leave open.

Align lower edge of piece 4 with dashed line on piece 3 for Extra Swingy Shoulder Bag.

City Roses Purse

Designed and made by Cassie Barden

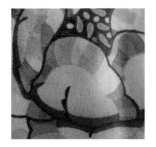

A wonderful showcase for your favorite fabrics, this is the perfect little purse and easier to make than it looks. The versatile shape works great with a range of personal styles, so after you've made bags for your niece and grandmother, make a couple for yourself! The pleats are a snap to stitch, and if you've never made custom-covered buttons before, they are shockingly easy and fun to make.

~Cassie

❀ **Finished purse: 16" x 9"** ❀

Materials

Yardage is based on 42"-wide fabric.

⅔ yard of cotton floral print for outside of bag and straps
⅜ yard of striped cotton fabric for lining and buttons
⅜ yard of 20"-wide medium-weight fusible interfacing
Magnetic purse closure
1 or 2 covered button kits, size ⅞"*

You will need enough to make 4 buttons.

Cutting

From the floral print, cut:
2 rectangles, 10" x 17"
2 strips, 5" x 24"

From the striped cotton fabric and interfacing, cut:
2 rectangles, 10" x 17", from each

Making the Purse

Use a ½" seam allowance unless otherwise specified.

1. Following the manufacturer's instructions, iron the interfacing to the wrong side of each of the two striped-lining rectangles.

2. Using the curve pattern on page 71, trace the pattern and cut out a template from plain paper, template plastic, or cardboard. Using the template, mark the curve on the bottom corners of each rectangle (both outer fabric and lining). Trim the corners. ①

3. Mark the pleat fold points along the top edge of each of the four rectangles, using the measurements shown. ②

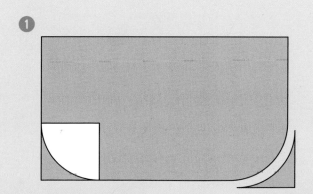

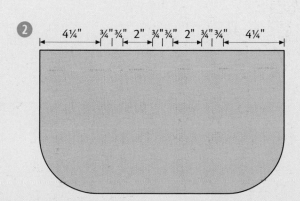

4. Press the pleats as shown, pressing the fold a little more than 2" down. On the wrong side of the fabric, draw a 2" line down from the top along each pleat fold, then stitch along the three lines as shown. Press the pleats flat in one direction. Repeat for each rectangle, including the lining. ③

5. Following the manufacturer's instructions, attach a magnetic closure to the lining pieces. Center the closures along the width (straddling each center-pleat fold) and place it 1" from the top raw edge as shown. ④

6. With right sides together and matching raw edges, sew the outer bag together around the sides and bottom, leaving the top open. Press all seams open as best you can, and clip the curves. Repeat with the two lining pieces, but leave a 4" opening on one side, backstitching on each side of this opening. ⑤

7. Turn the outer bag right side out, place inside the lining bag (right sides together), and match the top raw edges. Pin. Stitch around the entire top of the bag.

8. Turn the bag right side out by pulling it through the gap left in the lining. Nudge this top seam "open" by rolling it against your ironing board or on your knee, then press. Once you have a smooth, finished edge, topstitch around the top of the bag.

9. To make a strap, press a 5" x 24" floral-print strip in half lengthwise with wrong sides together. Then fold the long edges in toward this center crease and press again. ⑥

10. At each strap end, fold over one corner and then fold over the second corner to make a point. Secure the end and strap by topstitching a scant ⅛" from the edges around the entire perimeter of the strap. Repeat for the second strap. ⑦

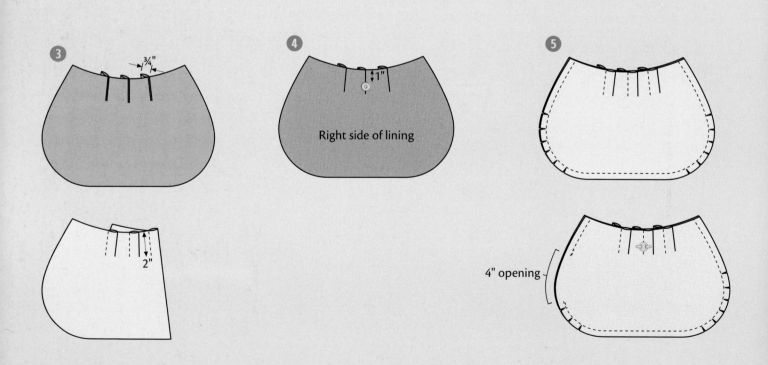

Right side of lining

2"

4" opening

11. Position the strap ends 1 ¼" from the side seams and 2" from the top edge, placing the folded ends against the bag. Stitch along the previous topstitching as shown through all layers to secure the straps to the bag. ⑧

12. Following the manufacturer's instructions, cover four ⅞" buttons with the striped lining fabric. Position each button as shown and stitch to the bag through all layers. ⑨

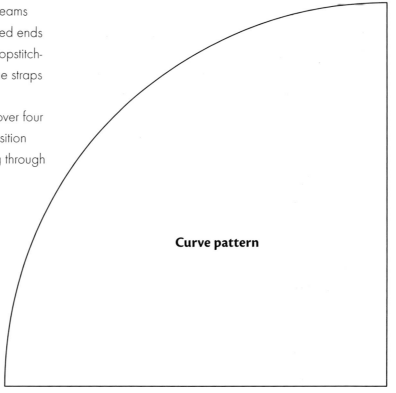

Curve pattern

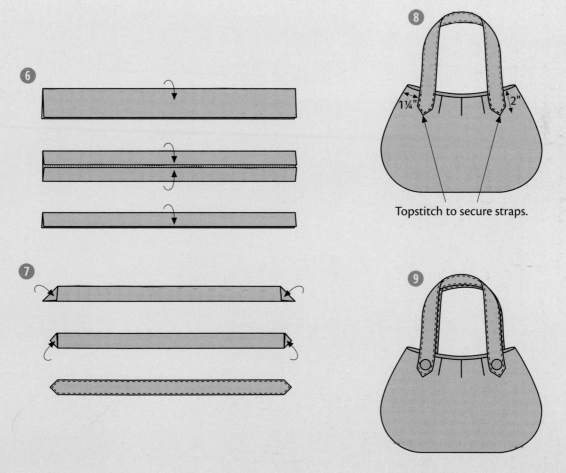

Topstitch to secure straps.

Dungaree Denim Scarf

Designed and made by Jenny Wilding Cardon

Got a "green" girl in your life? Give her a one-of-a-kind, show-stopping scarf—inspired by patched-up jeans and made from them, too! Softened denim, shiny satin brocade, and soft Minky combine for a wraparound fashion statement that's as cozy as it is cool. Choose satin squares that match the favorite colors of your eco-friendly trendsetter.

~Jenny

❀ **Finished size: 4½" x 69½"** ❀

Materials

Minky yardage is based on 58"-wide fabric; cotton yardage is based on 42"-wide fabric.

⅜ yard of medium-blue Minky fabric

⅜ yard of foundation fabric*

1 back pant leg from *each* of 5 different pairs of jeans, or ¼ yard *each* of 5 different hues of off-the-bolt denim (lights, mediums, and darks)

Scraps of 4 different satin-brocade fabrics, at least 2½" x 6"**

Scraps of lightweight fusible web, such as HeatnBond Lite

1½" square of cotton fabric for pressing

Denim sewing-machine needle

Thread to coordinate with denim colors

Large binder clip or bag clip (optional)

Long, blunt tool, such as a knitting needle

Seam ripper

You will sew the denim patches onto this fabric, and it won't be seen in the final scarf. Jenny used yardage from a 100% cotton secondhand sheet; you can use cotton, muslin, or any tightly woven fabric.

**Jenny used hot pink, dark purple, and two different blues. Use scraps from other sewing projects, or look for items such as women's blouses or men's ties at your favorite thrift store.*

Customize the Fabrics

Any color or style of Minky fabric will work well for this scarf. You can also use a number of different types of woven fabrics in place of the satin-brocade fabrics; try cotton prints, linen, felted wool, or even velvet. As long as the fabric is woven (not a stretchy knit) and can be used with fusible web, it will work.

Cutting

1. Cut the foundation fabric into 5"-wide strips, to make a total length of about 72". Piece the strips together along the 5" edges, using a ¼" seam allowance, to make a rectangle measuring 5" x 70". Press any seams open.

2. If you are using denim jeans, cut the fabric from one back pant leg of each pair. Leave pockets and any seams behind. ①

3. From each piece of denim, cut as many strips as you can from the length of the pant leg. Cut strips that are 2", 2½", and 3" wide.

4. Cut the Minky fabric into two 5"-wide strips. Piece the strips together using a ¼" seam allowance and trim to make a rectangle measuring 5" x 70".

Making the Scarf

1. Lay the 5" x 70" foundation fabric on a flat surface. Using a rotary cutter and mat or scissors, freehand cut a square or rectangle from one of the denim strips. Place the shape on top of one corner of the foundation fabric, aligning edges; pin in place. ②

2. Cut a different-size square or rectangle from a different-colored strip of denim. Place this shape next to the first shape, overlapping the edges of the two shapes by a generous ¼". Pin in place. Continue cutting and pinning shapes in differing sizes and colors until you have 10 to 15 patches pinned onto the foundation fabric. Make sure the foundation fabric is always completely hidden underneath your patches, and be sure all four edges of each patch cover adjacent patches by a generous ¼". ③

   Note: The squares and rectangles can vary in size from 1" to 3" in width and height. You can have short, fat squares; long, skinny rectangles; or any shape in between. It's important to vary the sizes of your shapes for a traditional "patchwork" effect.

3. Using coordinating thread and a denim machine-sewing needle, begin sewing each patch to the foundation fabric, folding patches back and moving pins as needed when sewing. Sew the underlying patches first; sew patches with fewer layers on top of them last. When sewing underlying layers, sew a scant ¼" from raw edges; when sewing top layers, sew a generous ¼" from raw edges. The idea is to capture the edges of each patch under the patch

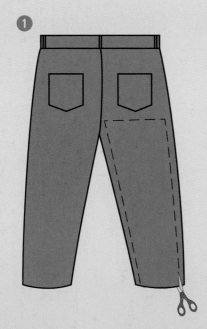

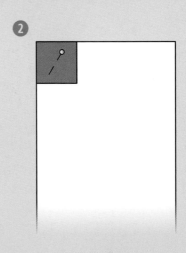

that lies on top of it, so all layers except the very top layer of patch edges are covered and stitched down. ④

> **Note:** There's no need to sew patches down along the foundation-fabric edges; just make sure the patches lie flat when sewn. Backstitch only when your stitching does not end at the edge of the foundation fabric.

4. Continue cutting, pinning, and sewing patches to the foundation fabric, 10 to 15 patches at a time, until you have covered the entire length of the foundation fabric with patches. If you have a binder clip, roll and secure the scarf ends to make sewing less awkward. When you have finished sewing the patches, flip the scarf over so the foundation fabric faces up. With rotary-cutting equipment or scissors, trim any overhanging patch fabric even with the foundation fabric.

5. Sew a machine-basting stitch along the edges of the foundation-pieced scarf.

6. Wash and dry your scarf by machine, using normal cycles. Cut away any long threads from the denim.

Embellishing with Colorful Patches

1. Adhere fusible web to the wrong side of the satin-brocade scraps, following the manufacturer's instructions. Cut the scraps into 1" squares. You can use any number of squares you wish; Jenny used 32 in her scarf:

Hot pink	11 squares
Dark purple	8 squares
Medium blue	7 squares
Light blue	6 squares

2. Lay the scarf flat on an ironing board, patch side up. Arrange each satin-brocade square where you like it along the scarf, making sure the squares are placed at least ½" from the scarf edges. Avoid placing the squares over the edges of the denim patches; instead, place them on flat areas. Place the 1½" square of cotton fabric over a satin-brocade square; fuse in place following the manufacturer's instructions. Repeat until all squares are fused. Take care not to place your iron over one square while you are pressing another; this can burn the satin-brocade fabric and gum up your iron. ⑤

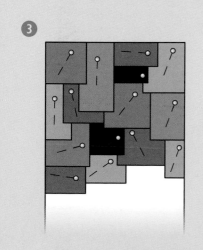

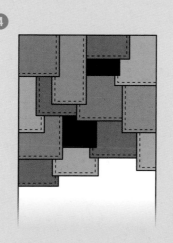

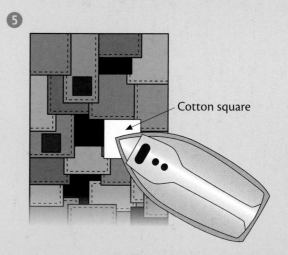

Cotton square

3. Set your machine to sew a tight zigzag stitch. Center the presser foot over one corner of a satin-brocade square. Stitch to the end of one side of the square. With the needle in the down position on the outer edge of the square, raise the presser foot and pivot the scarf 90° to sew the second side of the square. Lower the presser foot; then raise your needle to the center position using your hand wheel. Lift the presser foot again and reposition it so it is centered over the corner of the square. Lower the presser foot and stitch along the second side of the square. Repeat this two more times to zigzag stitch around the entire square. Backstitch and cut threads close to the stitching. Repeat until all satin-brocade squares are stitched to the scarf. ⑥

Completing the Scarf

1. Lay the scarf, right side up, on a flat surface. Place the 5" x 70" Minky rectangle, right side down, on top of the scarf; pin the edges well, keeping the raw edges aligned. Sew a ¼" seam around the entire scarf, leaving a 2" to 2½" opening at one short end of the scarf for turning. Backstitch at the beginning and end.

Pin for No-Slip Sewing

Minky fabrics can be slippery under your presser foot. The key to making it stay put? *Pin well*. Pin every 1½" to 2" to make sewing easier. You can also use a walking foot if you have one.

2. Push the scarf through the opening to turn it right side out. Using a long, blunt tool, such as a knitting needle or the eraser end of a pencil, push the four corners of the scarf outward into points. Roll the seams of the scarf on a flat surface to flatten the scarf along the edges. Turn the edges of the opening under ¼" and sew the opening closed using a whipstitch and coordinating thread.

3. Using the back edge of your seam ripper, rub the Minky fabric along the sewn seam with a light, quick back-and-forth motion to release the "fuzzies" in the fabric from the seam. This technique helps make the Minky fabric look plush around the sewn edge. ⑦

4. If needed or desired, you can flatten the scarf by pressing; use a pressing cloth and a dry iron. To shape the scarf even further, you can take two or three stitches just inside the seam along the long sides of the scarf, every 2" or so, to stabilize the layers.

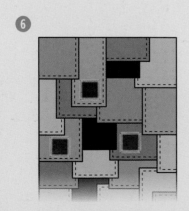

⑥

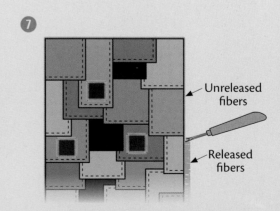

⑦

Unreleased fibers

Released fibers

Recycled-Wool Wristlet Purse and Companion Cup Cozy

Designed and made by Beth Kovich

Here's thrifty sophistication for the eco-savvy gal on the go! Quick-to-stitch recycled wool from just one thrift-store sweater makes the leap to a pair of essential, around-town accessories. Make the pair as a gift, and then make another duo for yourself.

~Beth

❀ **Finished purse size: 8" x 6½"** ❀

Materials for Wristlet and Cup Cozy

1 washed and fulled (felted) 100% wool knit sweater
    or equivalent

1 fat quarter of cotton print fabric

1 zipper, 9" long, to match sweater

1 D ring, 1" diameter

Assorted buttons, scraps, ribbon, and wool yarn
    for embellishments

¼ yard of Pellon Shape-Flex interfacing (optional)

Clean hot-beverage cup (model for Cup Cozy)

Cutting

From the body of the sweater, cut:

2 pieces, 8½" x 7", for purse exterior

From the lower ribbing of the sweater, cut:

1 piece, 2" x 18", for handle and tab

From the cotton fabric, cut:

2 pieces, 8½" x 7", for lining

From the interfacing (optional), cut:

2 pieces, 8" x 6½"

Making the Purse

1. If you are using interfacing, fuse it to the wrong side of the 8½" x 7" wool pieces, following the manufacturer's instructions.

2. Lay the 2" x 18" ribbing piece for the handle and tab, wrong side up, on a flat surface. Beginning at one short end, fold both long sides to the middle (bias-tape fashion) and pin along the entire length.

3. Prepare your sewing machine for a wide, short zigzag stitch (width at 6, length at 2 works well) and use thread to match the exterior fabric. Place the handle under the presser foot and stitch down the center of the strip for the entire length to join the butted, raw edges. The zigzag stitch should catch both cut edges. Press gently if necessary. ①

4. Cut one 12" piece for the purse handle and one 4" piece for the tab from the strip made in step 3.

5. Layer one of the lining pieces and one of the wool pieces, right sides together. Position the zipper between the two pieces along the top 8½" edge. (The zipper will be longer than your cut pieces; position the zipper pull at one end and let the excess extend beyond the other side.) Make sure the right side of the zipper is facing the wool fabric. If your lining fabric is directional, pay careful attention at this step so that it will be oriented the way you want it. Pin the edges. Using a zipper foot, sew along the edge to attach the zipper. Repeat this step with the other side. Press seam allowances away from the zipper.

Tips for Working with Recycled Wool

- When raiding your closet or shopping for a sweater, read the fabric labels and look for garments that are *at least* 85% wool as they will offer the best results when fulled (aka felted) by laundering. Sweaters rich in cashmere, alpaca, angora, and mohair offer good results, too. Usually, Beth's favorite sweater finds are 100% lambswool.

- Prepare your sweater by machine washing with a small amount of detergent, hot water, and a cool rinse. Add a couple of old towels to increase agitation and speed up the fulling process. Machine dry on low setting. Results will vary depending upon fiber content and the knit pattern of the garment. Repeat the process to further full the knitwear.

- Any flaws present on the garment before washing will still exist after washing. Don't despair! Cover any holes or spots with a decorative patch, button, or novelty stitching, and voilà, you have a piece of designer knitwear to work with. You may have enough fabric to work around imperfections as well.

- If you're lucky enough to have a stash of reclaimed knitwear, smaller pieces may be stitched together crazy-quilt style to obtain the size necessary for this project. Be sure to use a wide zigzag stitch (Beth uses W6, L2 on her machine) to securely stitch the butted, cut edges together. Press gently with a steam iron from the wrong side to regain shape after joining. Assemble a patchwork of fabric larger than the required size and trim to the project measurements.

- Knits can be stretchy even after felting, so use a slightly longer stitch length and a ⅜" seam allowance for piecing (½" if bulky). Work slowly and pin thoroughly for optimal results.

- The gusseted purse will get most of its shape from the knitwear you use, so softer knits can make for a somewhat slouchy wristlet. If you prefer a bag that stands on its own, select a firmer knit or reinforce lighter-weight wools with an interfacing such as Pellon Shape-Flex (item SF101), an all-purpose, woven fusible interfacing. Simply iron it to the wrong side of the knitwear, following the manufacturer's instructions, before assembly.

- Always iron from the wrong side of the wool or use a pressing cloth. Use the wool setting on your iron with steam.

6. Fold the 4" tab piece in half and place the D ring in the fold. Position the folded tab on the right side of the wool at the end of the zipper (opposite the zipper pull). Offset the ends of the tab to minimize bulk, letting the ends extend beyond the wool piece; pin in place approximately 1" below the zipper and baste. ②

7. Fold the 12" handle piece in half and position it along the side seam approximately 1" below the zipper pull. Arrange the ends of the handle in a single layer, pin, and baste. Open the zipper three-quarters of the way. This will allow you to turn the bag right side out when you are finished sewing the outer edges. It's magical. ③

8. Place the two wool rectangles with right sides together and the two lining sections right sides together. Pin around the edges very securely, paying careful attention to aligning the open ends of the zipper. Along the side seams, finger-press the bulk of the zipper and the wool layers toward the lining fabric.

9. Mark a 4" opening along the bottom seam of the lining fabric to allow turning after stitching.

10. Using a ⅜" (or ½" if very bulky) seam allowance and a regular presser foot, stitch around the piece, leaving the opening in the lining fabric. Sew a second row of stitching at the handle and tab intersections to reinforce these areas. Use caution and sew slowly when sewing over the zipper—sewing fast is an easy way to break a needle!

11. To create a gusseted bottom for the wristlet, finger-press the seam allowances open and match up the bottom and side seams at one corner. Pin in place and sew across each corner in a straight line 1¼" from the point (on the wool corners use two rows of stitching for strength). Trim the excess fabric ⅜" from the stitching line. Repeat with the remaining three corners. ④

12. Trim excess bulk from the handle, tab, and zipper area.

13. Turn the purse right side out, leaving the lining extended. Sew the lining opening closed with a slip stitch and tuck the lining into the bag.

14. Close the zipper and embellish the bag using wool scraps, ribbon, and buttons as desired.

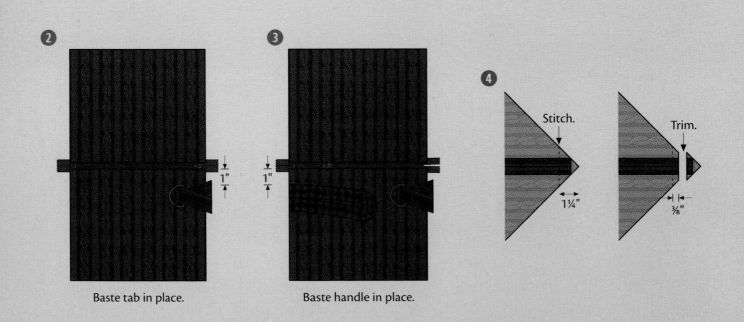

② Baste tab in place.

③ Baste handle in place.

④ Stitch. 1¼" Trim. ⅜"

Cup Cozy (bonus project)

This is the easiest low-sew gift you'll ever make! It's a nice, reusable alternative to the cardboard sleeves you pick up at the coffee shop. To make this project, you'll need a good-sized sweater with sleeves that stay stretchy after washing. The cup cozy must be able to easily slip on and off a cup of hot coffee safely.

1. Using sturdy scissors, remove a sleeve from the washed sweater along the shoulder seam.

2. Leave the sleeve intact, in a "tube" shape. Check the sizing by sliding a paper hot-beverage cup (bottom first, no handle) into the large end of the sleeve and pushing it down toward the cuff. If the bottom of the cup peeks out of the cuff without too much resistance, you're in luck! If it doesn't, you'll need to try another sweater. ⑤

3. Remove the cup and lay the sleeve on a flat surface. Using a ruler, measure up 6" from the bottom edge of the cuff and mark a cutting line with straight pins. Make the cut.

4. Fold the top edge down twice, approximately ½" to ¾" each time, and pin in place. Secure the hem by tacking in place by hand with matching thread or working a blanket stitch in wool yarn along the edge (as shown in the photograph on page 77). Be careful not to draw the stitches up too tightly. Refer to "Blanket Stitch" on page 106 for additional details if needed. ⑥

5. Add buttons or other embellishment as desired.

This little purse looks good in any color.

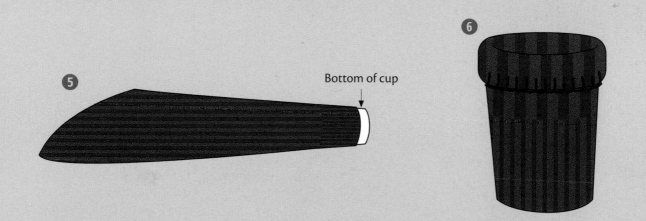

⑤

Bottom of cup

⑥

Lunch-Break Reusable Bags

Designed and made by Sara Diepersloot

Make a statement and take your lunch break in style with this reusable lunch and sandwich/snack-bag set. These make excellent gifts for kids, friends, family, or coworkers. Simply wipe the vinyl lining clean, or toss in the washing machine.

~Sara

Finished lunch bag: 8½" x 10½" x 4" ❀ **Finished sandwich/snack bag: 5¾" x 6¼" x 1½"**

Materials

Yardage is based on 42"-wide fabric and 54"-wide vinyl.

⅝ yard of blue-and-green floral for lunch bag and sandwich bag

½ yard of navy floral for lunch-bag lining

⅜ yard or 1 fat quarter of white-and-blue polka-dot fabric for lunch bag

¼ yard of green striped fabric for lunch bag

¼ yard of canvas for lunch-bag handles

½ yard of 16-gauge clear vinyl for lunch-bag lining

⅓ yard of 12-gauge clear vinyl for sandwich-bag lining

2 lengths of Velcro, ½" x 6", for lunch bag and sandwich bag

Tips for Working with Clear Vinyl

- If you find it difficult to sew on the vinyl, simply lay a piece of tracing paper between the vinyl and the sewing-machine presser foot to prevent the foot from sticking to the vinyl as you sew.
- When ironing these projects, do not place the iron directly on the vinyl; instead, use a pressing cloth.

Cutting

From the blue-and-green floral, cut:

2 rectangles, 8" x 13½", for lunch bag

1 rectangle, 8¾" x 16½", for sandwich bag

From the green striped fabric, cut:

2 rectangles, 1¼" x 13½", for lunch bag

1 strip, 3½" x 44"; crosscut into 2 pieces, 3½" x 21", for lunch bag

From the white-and-blue polka-dot fabric, cut:

1 rectangle, 10½" x 13½", for lunch bag

From the navy floral, cut:

1 rectangle, 13½" x 27", for lunch bag

From the canvas, cut:

1 strip, 3½" x 44"; crosscut into 2 pieces, 3½" x 21", for lunch bag

From the 16-gauge clear vinyl, cut:

1 rectangle, 13½" x 27", for lunch bag

From the 12-gauge clear vinyl, cut:

1 rectangle, 8¾" x 16½", for sandwich bag

Making the Lunch Bag

Use ¼" seam allowances throughout unless otherwise indicated.

1. Sew one 8" x 13½" blue-and-green floral rectangle to one 1¼" x 13½" green striped rectangle. Press. Make two. ①

2. Sew each unit to one 13½" side of the white-and-blue polka-dot rectangle. Press. ②

3. Fold the bag right sides together. Sew along both sides using a ½" seam allowance. Press the seam allowances open. ③

4. Press the bottom corners of the bag flat as shown. Measure 2" down from each corner and draw a line with your ruler. Sew on this line. Trim away the excess, leaving ½" beyond the stitching line. ④

5. Lay the clear vinyl 13½" x 27" rectangle on top of the *right* side of the navy floral rectangle for the lining. Stitch ¼" from each 27" side to hold the layers together. ⑤

6. Fold the lining right sides together. Sew along both sides using a ½" seam allowance and leaving a 5" opening on one of the sides for turning. Press the seam allowances open.

7. Repeat step 4 for the bag lining.

8. Layer one canvas piece and one 3½" x 21" green striped handle piece *wrong* sides together. Press under a ½" seam allowance along each of the 21" sides. Press the strip in half lengthwise with *wrong* sides together. Topstitch a scant ⅛" from each edge of the handle. Make two handles. ⑥

9. Measure 3½" from the side seams of the outer bag and mark. Center the ends of the handles over the marks and pin in place, making sure the handles are not twisted. Stitch across the handles ¼" from the

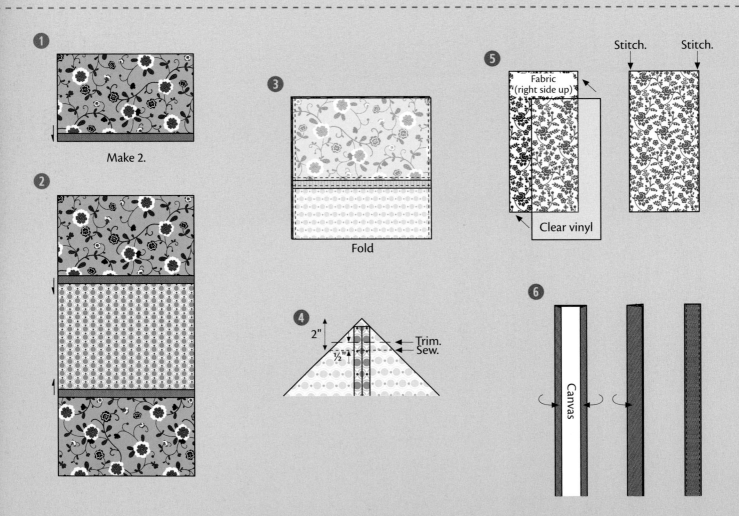

① Make 2.

③ Fold

④ 2" ½" Trim. Sew.

⑤ Fabric (right side up) Clear vinyl Stitch. Stitch.

⑥ Canvas

top edge of the bag to hold the ends in place until the lining is sewn in. ⑦

10. Place the outer bag inside of the lining, right sides together. Matching side seams, pin the top edges together. Sew around the top edge using a ½" seam allowance.

11. Turn the bag right side out through the opening in the lining. Press. Stitch the opening in the lining closed.

12. Center a 6" piece of Velcro inside the lunch bag ½" from the top edge on both sides. Topstitch in place. ⑧

Making the Sandwich Bag

1. Lay the 8¾" x 16½" clear vinyl rectangle on the *wrong* side of the 8¾" x 16½" blue-and-green

floral rectangle. Fold over ¼" on each of the 8¾" ends. Fold over again 1" and press. Topstitch. ⑨

2. Center a 6" Velcro piece on each of the folded-fabric ends. Topstitch. ⑩

3. Fold the sandwich bag in half, *wrong* sides together. Sew the side seams with a ¼" seam allowance.

4. Turn the bag inside out. Finger-press flat. Sew the side seams again using a ½" seam allowance. This will enclose your seams and make for a nice, smooth bag that is easy to clean.

5. While the bag is still inside out, press the bottom corners of the bag flat as shown in step 4 for the lunch bag. Measure ¾" from each corner and draw a line with your ruler. Sew on this line. Trim the excess, leaving ½" beyond the stitching line. ⑪

6. Turn the sandwich bag right side out and enjoy!

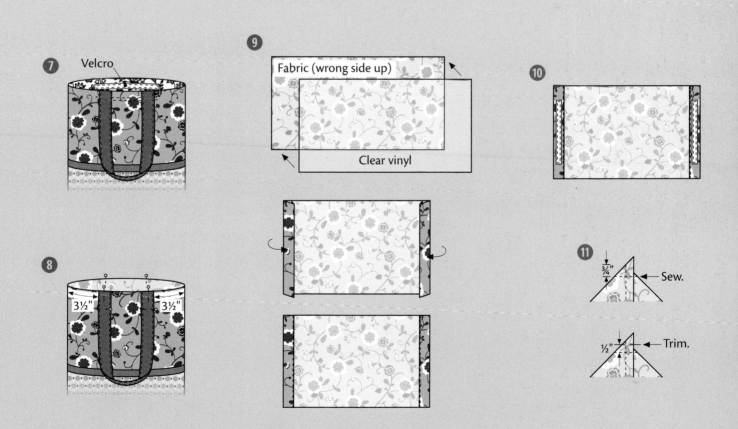

Little Wool Bags

Designed and made by Karen Clifton

I had an "aha" moment when I realized that instead of using a gift bag to hold a present, I could make the bag be part of the gift. Or it could be the gift itself! Making larger wool appliqué projects left me with lots of great scraps and inspired the design ideas used in these clever and fun little bags. Selecting from wool pennies, flowers, folk-art stars, or even quilt-pattern motifs makes each bag an opportunity to let a sense of play, color, and design emerge.

~Karen

Petal-Pusher Bag

❀ **Finished size: 5" x 4½"** ❀

Materials

See page 107 for instructions on felting wool.

5" x 12" piece of white felted wool for bag*
4" x 4" square of purple felted wool for flower
2" x 2" square of orange felted wool for flower center
2" x 3" piece of green felted wool for leaves
Freezer paper for templates
Glue stick
Black #8 pearl cotton
1"-diameter purple button

Karen suggests heavy, jacket-weight wool for the bag. Any weight will be fine for the appliqué.

Tracing and Cutting

1. Using the patterns on page 91, trace the flower, flower center, and two leaves onto freezer paper. Cut the templates a little beyond the tracing lines.

2. Iron the templates onto the wool as follows: iron the flower template onto the purple wool, the flower-center template onto the orange wool, and the leaf templates onto the green wool.

3. Cut out each template on the drawn lines. Remove the paper from the wool.

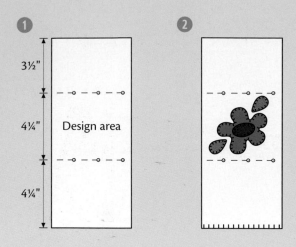

3½"

4¼" Design area

4¼"

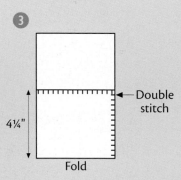

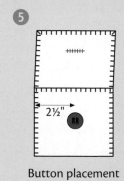

Double stitch ←

4¼"

Fold

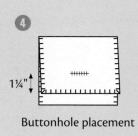

1¼"

Buttonhole placement

5

2½"

Button placement

Assembling the Bag

1. Lay the piece of white wool on your worktable, with the 12" sides running vertically, and mark off the design area where the appliqué will be sewn. Measure down 3½" from the top and mark with a few straight pins. Measure up 4¼" from the bottom and mark with a few straight pins. ①

2. Dab a bit of glue on the wrong side of the flower center and position it in the center of the flower. Using a single strand of pearl cotton, blanket stitch around the flower center, referring to "Blanket Stitch" on page 106 for additional details if needed.

3. Position the flower and leaves on the white wool in the design area between the pins as desired. Remember to allow space along the side edges for blanket stitching.

4. When you are pleased with the arrangement, dab a bit of glue on the back of each appliqué and glue into position. Using a single strand of pearl cotton, blanket stitch around the flower and two leaves.

5. Using a double strand of pearl cotton, blanket stitch across the bottom (5") side of the white wool. ②

6. Turn the white wool over and using the lower row of pins as your guide, fold the bottom up along the pin line to create a pocket 4¼" deep. Pin along the sides to hold the pocket in place.

7. Starting on one side at the bottom and using a double strand of pearl cotton, blanket stitch the side of the pocket, stitching through both layers of wool. At the top of the pocket, use the last stitch on the opening edge as a guide and reinforce the opening by taking a double stitch. ③

8. Continue blanket stitching up the side, across the top, and down the other side. Be sure to double stitch at the top of the pocket on the other side.

Finishing the Bag

1. Fold the top down along the upper pin line to create a flap. On the outside flap, measure 1¼" from the edge and mark a 1" long buttonhole, centering it from side to side. Cut the buttonhole open and sew around the opening by hand using a buttonhole stitch. Refer to "Buttonhole Stitch" on page 106 for further details if needed. ④

   Note: The stitching around the buttonhole adds a nice finishing touch, but it isn't absolutely necessary, as the felted wool will not fray.

2. Fold the flap down and mark the spot for the button. It should be 2½" from each side. Sew the button in place to correspond with the buttonhole. ⑤

3. Complete your bag by giving it a good steaming. Wet and wring out a terry-cloth towel or dishcloth. Place your wool bag on an ironing board, cover it with the damp cloth, and place a hot, dry iron on the cloth. Allow the steam to rise. Move the iron around the cloth as necessary until the entire bag has been steamed. Flip the bag over and repeat the process. Allow the bag to dry flat.

Mix It Up!

Don't be afraid to incorporate new as well as recycled felted wool in these bags. You'll have more choices in fabric weight, colors, and weaves, all of which can lead to interesting design options.

Dotz

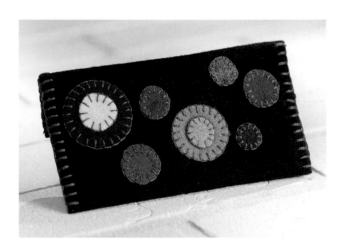

Materials

See page 107 for instructions on felting wool.

6" x 16" piece of purple felted wool for bag*
Assorted 2" square scraps of different-colored felted wool for appliqués
Freezer paper for templates
Glue stick
Yellow #8 pearl cotton
½"-diameter button

Karen suggests heavy, jacket-weight wool for the bag. Any weight will be fine for the appliqués.

Tracing and Cutting

1. Trace the following circles onto freezer paper:
   - 1 circle each of 1⅞", 1½", ¾", and ½" diameters
   - 3 circles, ⅞" diameter
   - 2 circles, ⅝" diameter

2. Cut out the templates just outside the tracing lines and iron them onto the assorted scraps of wool, keeping in mind value and contrast.

3. Cut out each circle on the drawn line and remove the freezer paper.

Assembling the Bag

1. Using a small dab of glue, center a ⅞" circle on top of the 1⅞" circle. Glue one of the ⅝" circles in the center of the 1½" circle. Blanket stitch the small circles in place.

2. Lay the purple wool on your work surface with the long edges vertical. Mark off the design area where the appliqué will be sewn: measure 2¾" up from the bottom edge of the wool and mark with a few straight pins. Measure up another 3¼" from that pin and mark with a few more pins. ①

3. Arrange the wool circles within the design area. Be sure to allow about ½" of space along the side edges for blanket stitching. When you are pleased with the positioning, dab a bit of glue on the back of each piece and glue in place.

4. Using a single strand of pearl cotton, blanket stitch around each circle.

5. Fold the wool in half, with the appliqué facing out. Using a double strand of pearl cotton, blanket stitch along the 6"-wide bottom edge, sewing through both layers of purple wool.

6. Turn the wool over so the appliqués are face down. With the fold at the top and the stitched edge at the bottom, fold the bottom up along the pin line to create a pocket that's about 2¾" deep.

7. Using a double strand of pearl cotton, start at one bottom corner and blanket stitch along the entire side, sewing through all layers. At the top of the pocket, use the last stitch on the opening edge as a guide and reinforce the opening by taking a double stitch to reinforce the pocket corner. Continue blanket stitching up the side to the top fold. ②

8. Blanket stitch along the opposite side in the same manner, remembering to double stitch at the top of the pocket.

Finishing the Bag

1. Fold the top edge of the pocket down along the upper pin line to create a flap. On the outside flap, measure ¾" up from the lower edge and mark a ½"-long buttonhole in the center of the flap. Cut the buttonhole open and buttonhole stitch around the opening if desired.

2. Fold the flap down and mark the button placement. Sew the button in place to correspond with the buttonhole.

3. Complete your bag by giving it a good steaming, following step 3 of "Finishing the Bag" for the Petal-Pusher Bag on page 89.

Make a bag in whatever size, shape, or color suits your fancy.

Tips for Cutting Circles

- A plastic Combo Circle template from an office-supply store is great for tracing precise circle shapes onto freezer paper.

- To ensure smooth edges when cutting circles out of wool, hold the scissors in place and rotate the template or wool as you cut.

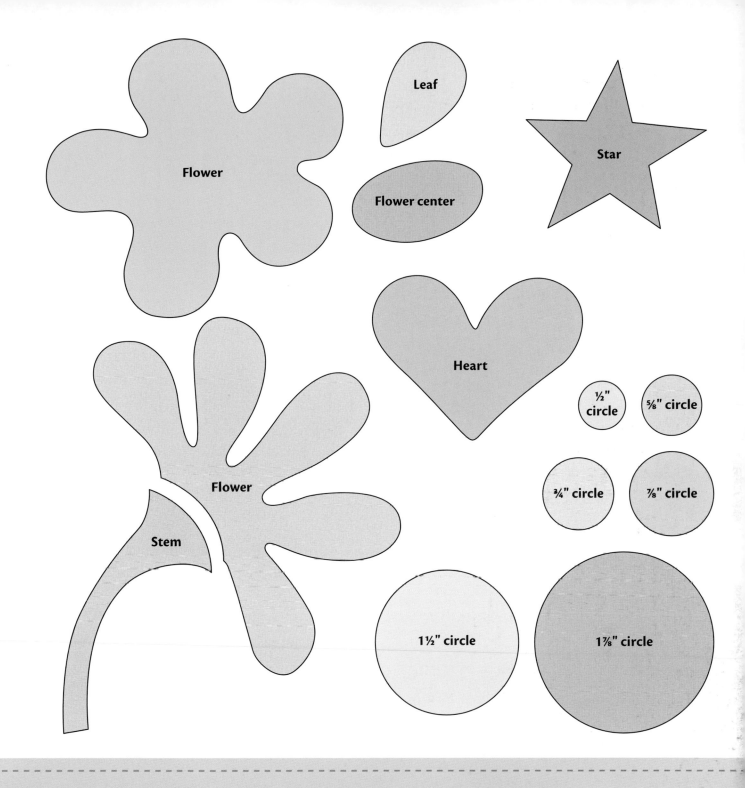

Flower

Leaf

Star

Flower center

Heart

Flower

Stem

½" circle

⅝" circle

¾" circle

⅞" circle

1½" circle

1⅞" circle

① 2¾"   3¼"

Design area

② Fold

2¾"

Double stitch

Squarely in the Round Wool Bracelets

Designed and made by Karen Clifton

Inspired by a bracelet that was made from cardboard circles (funky, but very cool!), I thought it might be possible to do something similar with felted wool. The result—these easy, fun, woolly wristbands.

~Karen

❀ **Finished size: 7½" circumference** ❀

Materials

See page 107 for instructions on felting wool.

2" x 10" piece of white felted wool
2" x 10" piece of black felted wool
1" x 10" piece of red felted wool
1" x 10" piece of gray felted wool
18" of .5mm elastic jewelry cord
42 red size 6/0 beads
Beading needle

Cutting

Use a rotary cutter or scissors to cut the wool.

From each of the white and black wool pieces, cut:
14 squares, ⅝" x ⅝"

From each of the red and gray wool pieces, cut:
7 squares, ⅝" x ⅝"

Design Options

The instructions are for a red, white, gray, and black bracelet, but you can use any colors you like. Or you can cut circles instead of squares. Or combine circles and squares. It's fun to try different shapes and color combinations so you can make bracelets for all your friends with no two being exactly alike.

Assembling the Bracelet

These bracelets were made using an alternating pattern of A and B units. You'll need seven of each unit, with a bead between each square.

- Unit A: white-gray-black squares
- Unit B: white-red-black squares ①

1. Using the 18" length of jewelry cord, thread your needle and knot the end.

2. Begin with a unit A: Push the needle through the center of a white square and move the square down the cord. Add a bead. Thread on a gray square and add a bead. Thread on a black square and add a bead.

3. Now add a unit B: white square, bead, red square, bead, black square, bead.

4. Continue to thread the squares and beads onto the cord, alternating between unit A and unit B, with a bead between each square, until all the squares are threaded on to the cord, ending with a bead. ②

Completing the Bracelet

1. Remove the needle and gently move all the squares and beads to the center of the cord. Adjust the squares and beads to be gently touching but not crowded.

2. Bring the ends of the cord together, forming a circle. Gently pulling on the cord until the beginning white square nestles up to the last red bead, tie a square knot (left end over right, and then right end over left).

3. Trim the cord close to the knot. Slide the trimmed ends of the cord inside the red bead.

Don't Stop There

Make your gift extra special by sewing a little wool bag (page 86) to put the bracelet in. Or make a coordinating wristlet purse (page 77).

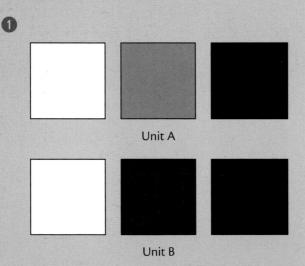

Unit A

Unit B

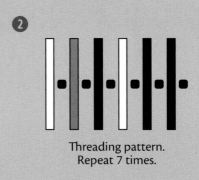

Threading pattern.
Repeat 7 times.

We Three Trees Quilt

Designed and made by Sarah Bisel

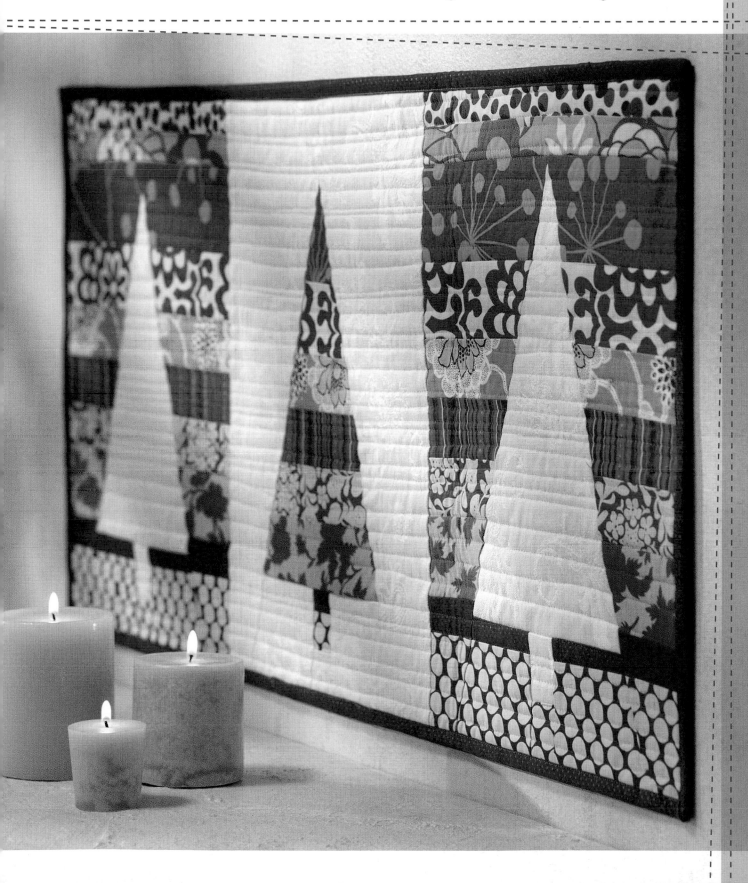

Sometimes we want to shake up the normal Christmas decorations with something modern, bright, and spunky. These trees will make you smile every time you look at them because they are unexpected, yet still sing a Christmas tune!

~Sarah

❀ **Finished size: 34" x 16¾"** ❀

Materials (for two wall hangings)

Yardage is based on 42"-wide fabric.

⅛ yard *each* of 7 different red prints for trees
⅛ yard *each* of 3 different bright green prints for trees
⅝ yard of white solid for background
¾ yard of red print for binding
1 yard of fabric for backing
Freezer paper
2 pieces of batting, 20" x 38"

Cutting

From the red prints for trees, cut a *total* of:
2 strips, 1½" x 42"
2 strips, 2" x 42"
1 strip, 2½" x 42"
1 strip, 3" x 42"
1 strip, 3½" x 42"

From the green prints, cut a *total* of:
1 strip, 1½" x 42"
1 strip, 2" x 42"
1 strip, 2½" x 42"

From the white solid, cut:
1 piece, 17" x 42"

From the red print for binding, cut:
6 strips, 2½" x 42"

Piecing the Tree Blocks

1. Draw a cutting diagram on a 14" x 17½" piece of freezer paper using the measurements shown. ①

2. Sew the red print and green print strips together in the order shown in the illustration. Press the seam allowances in one direction. ②

3. Layer the pieced strip and white piece together, right sides facing up, and cut into three 14" segments.

   Note: If your strips are shorter than 42", measure the length, divide by three, and cut the segments to that measurement.

4. Layer all the 14" segments to create one stack, alternating the white and pieced segments.

5. Remove the top segment and iron the freezer paper to the right side. Place it back on top of the stack.

6. Cut through all layers of the stack using a ruler and rotary cutter, following the numerical cutting order shown in the diagram. ③

7. Carefully remove the freezer-paper pieces from the top layer, and move the tree (E) and tree trunk (A) pieces to the bottom of the stack.

8. Remove the sections of the top layer and sew the tree block together in alphabetical order: sew A to B, then AB to C, then ABC to D, then ABCD to E, then ABCDE to F, then ABCDEF to G. Press all seam allowances away from the tree. *When piecing, take care to line up the seams of the strips in the pieced F and G sections. There will be some crazy seams, and that is okay.*

9. Repeat the sewing for each layer of the stack.
10. When all of the blocks are complete, simply square up each block to the same size, approximately 12" x 16¾".

Putting It All Together

This is the fun part. You get to decide how to sew the blocks together. Place three trees in a row horizontally, or if you have a narrow wall you want to decorate, piece them together vertically. These instructions make six trees, so you can create a number of small quilts as gifts. Other suggestions of items you could make are: place mats, wall hangings, door decorations, a lap quilt, table runner, pillow, or whatever else you can imagine!

Completing the Quilt

Refer to the quilting and binding techniques found on pages 105–109 for details as needed. The trees shown were quilted with random straight-line quilting, giving this quick quilt an extra-modern touch.

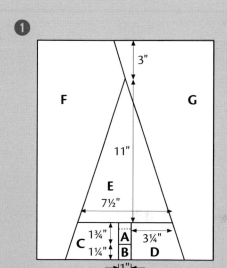

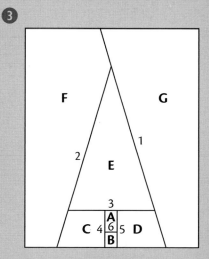

Poinsettia Table Runner

Designed and made by Karen Costello Soltys

Who would guess that this Christmas table runner is as quick and easy to make as it is elegant? You can stitch one up in no time for a lovely hostess gift or for anyone on your holiday gift list.

~ Karen

❀ **Finished size: 17½" x 41"** ❀

Materials

Yardage is based on 42"-wide fabric.

1 yard of light green print for table runner and backing

2¼ yards of ⅜"-wide red ribbon*

20" x 44" piece of low-loft batting or fusible fleece

2¼ yards of ⅜"-wide fusible web, such as HeatnBond or Stitch Witchery

½ yard of 20"-wide fusible web

4 silk poinsettia blossoms

Gold heat-set crystals, seed beads, or buttons for poinsettia centers

Parchment paper

*Karen used a glitter ribbon, but grosgrain or velvet ribbons work well, too.

Quilting the Table Runner

1. Cut the light green print in half crosswise to make two pieces, approximately 18" x 42". Remove the selvages and layer the fabric pieces, right sides together, on top of the batting. If you're using fusible fleece, fuse it to the wrong side of one of the green fabric pieces, then layer the other piece on top. Pin the layers together around the perimeter.

2. Starting on one short end about 1" from a corner, sew around the perimeter of the layers using a ¼" seam allowance and stopping after you sew about 1" past the last corner. Leave the rest of this short end open for turning. A walking foot is helpful for this step if you have one. ①

3. Trim the excess batting and clip the corners. Turn the table runner right side out and press flat, turning in the raw edges at the open end. Topstitch ¼" from the edge all around the table runner to ensure the edges won't roll. Then edgestitch around the runner. This will secure the open end.

4. Quilt the center of the table runner as desired. Karen quilted the one shown in an allover meander pattern.

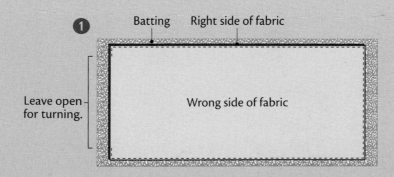

❶   Batting   Right side of fabric

Leave open for turning.

Wrong side of fabric

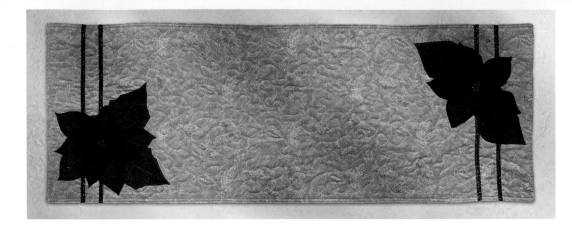

Embellishing the Table Runner

1. Cut four lengths of ribbon about 19" long. Peel the paper off one side of the ⅜"-wide fusible web and position the adhesive side down on the wrong side of the ribbon. Fuse in place. (If you're using Stitch Witchery that doesn't have paper, place parchment paper over the ribbon and fusible product so that it won't adhere to your iron.)

2. Using a rotary-cutting ruler as a guide, measure 3" from one short end of the table runner and align one length of ribbon against the ruler. Remove the ruler and fuse in place, folding the ribbon under at each end so that the ends align with the edges of the table runner. These ends will be stitched in place later. Position a second ribbon 1½" from the first and fuse in the same manner. Machine stitch close to the ribbon edges using matching thread to secure.

3. Repeat step 2 on the other end of the table runner.

4. To make the poinsettia appliqués, peel the silk flower petals from the plastic stems, peeling from the stem end out toward the end of the petal. At the ironing board, position the petals on the adhesive side of the fusible web, grouping the petals for each flower so that you can keep them organized.

5. Place the parchment paper over the top to protect your iron from the exposed adhesive. (If you're using Steam-A-Seam, you won't need parchment, as it has paper on both sides. Simply peel the paper off one side, position the petals right side up, and then replace the paper layer over the top.) Fuse, referring to the manufacturer's instructions and taking care not to scorch the petals.

Fuse Lightly!

To prevent scorching, fuse for a just a second or two from the top, then carefully flip all of the petal and paper layers over and fuse again from the back. That's the side where the adhesive is, which means it adheres more quickly to the petals this way. And you won't have to use a hot iron for too long on the delicate petals.

6. Once the fusible web has cooled, cut out around the perimeter of each petal. If any of the petals have frayed a bit, simply trim off the frayed edges. Working with the petals for one flower at a time, peel the paper backing from the petals and position the petals onto the table runner, referring to the photo above for placement. When satisfied, fuse in place. You may want to use a scrap of fabric as a press cloth to protect the silk petals from the hot iron.

7. Repeat step 6 for each additional flower. You can overlap them for a more natural arrangement, or place them however you like.

8. When all of the flowers are fused in place, add the heat-set crystals for the stamens, or hand stitch seed beads in the flower centers. Another option is to sew yellow or gold buttons in the flower centers.

Elegant Parsons Chair Dressing

Designed and made by Avis Shirer

I have plain black-leather Parsons chairs in my dining room. I love their simple elegance and graceful lines. Sometimes, though, it's fun to dress them up, and these clever and unique little quilts simply tie on. These would look wonderful on every chair in the dining room; or just go for two—one on each end of the table. The big bows make them very festive, and the glittery rickrack adds the bling.

~Avis

❀ **Finished size: 12½" x 42"** ❀

Materials for 2 Chair Covers

Yardage is based on 42"-wide fabric.

2¼ yards of very light green print for background and backing

2⅛ yards of green polka-dot fabric for binding and ties

⅓ yard of red solid or print for poinsettias

Scrap of gold print for poinsettia centers

7 yards of 1⅞"-wide metallic green rickrack

36 to 40 assorted green buttons for embellishing poinsettias

2 pieces of batting, 18" x 42"

1 yard of 18"-wide fusible web

Cutting for 2 Chair Covers

From the light green print, cut:

4 pieces, 18" x 42"

From the green polka-dot fabric, cut:

8 strips, 6½" x 42"

6 strips, 2½" x 42"

Making the Chair Covers

1. Layer the batting between two of the 18" x 42" light green pieces and baste for quilting.

2. Quilt as desired. Avis quilted in an allover stipple pattern, but 45° cross-hatching or another overall design would work well, too. Trim the quilted piece to 12½" x 42" or to the size that best fits your chairs. ①

3. Stitch the 2½"-wide green polka-dot binding strips together to make one long continuous strip. Sew the binding to the right side of the piece, but don't turn it to the back yet or hand stitch it.

4. Fold a 6½" x 42" green polka-dot strip in half lengthwise, right sides together, to make a tie. Stitch the long raw edges together and stitch across one short end. Leave the other end open and turn the tube right side out. Press well. Make four ties. ②

5. Fold the unsewn end of the ties to create a pleat, making them about 1½" wide. ③

6. Position the ties on the long side of the chair cover, ¾" from each corner, and sew them in the binding seam. Turn the binding to the back and slipstitch in place. ④

7. Repeat steps 1–6 to make a second chair cover.

Adding Rickrack and Appliqués

1. Cut four strips of rickrack approximately 46" long. Fold under the raw edge of the rickrack; aligning the curves to make an invisible beginning. Pin one length of rickrack next to the binding on the long side of the chair cover. Trim and fold back the rickrack again on the opposite end to hide the raw edge. ⑤

2. Using matching thread, machine stitch the rickrack in place, stitching along both sides. Repeat these steps for the remaining 46" strips of rickrack. ⑥

3. Cut four strips of rickrack 16½" long. Place one length of rickrack 1½" from the binding along each short side, pin, and stitch as you did before to attach the rickrack. ⑦

4. Using the poinsettia pattern on page 104, trace it onto the paper side of the fusible web four times, leaving about ½" between each pattern. Referring

to the manufacturer's instructions for the fusible web, fuse to the wrong side of the red poinsettia fabric. Cut out the appliqués and fuse in place. Machine stitch around each appliqué using a blanket stitch and matching thread.

5. Prepare the gold flower centers and appliqué using your favorite method.

6. Add green buttons to the flower centers. Tie to your chair and enjoy!

Types of quilting

Fold edge under.

1½"

¾" ¾"

Backing side

1½"

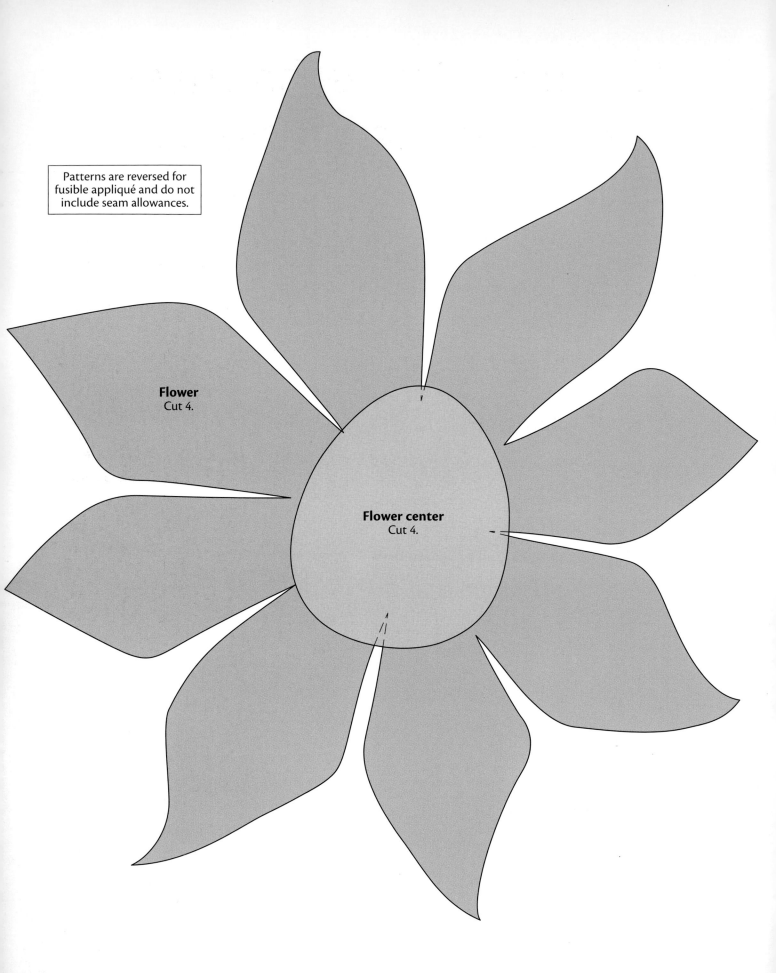

Patterns are reversed for fusible appliqué and do not include seam allowances.

Flower
Cut 4.

Flower center
Cut 4.

Basic Sewing Techniques— An Illustrated Glossary

Most of the projects in this book are relatively easy to make. But if any of the sewing language is unfamiliar, the information provided here may clear things up for you.

Binding

Narrow fabric strips folded over raw edges of projects—such as quilts, purse pockets, and more—are called binding. Binding is used to encase and finish edges, especially where there are multiple layers of fabrics and batting, as on a quilt. Binding strips are cut anywhere from 2" to 2½" wide, depending on the individual quilter's preference and on how thick the batting is.

Fold binding strips in half lengthwise with right sides together. Stitch them to the edge of the project from the right side of the project. Fold the binding strip up at a 45° angle when you reach a corner, and then fold it back down along the next edge of the project and continue sewing. ①

When you near the starting point, overlap the beginning and ending tails of the binding. Mark the overlap by the same distance as the width of your binding strips. (If your strips are 2½" wide, then mark the overlap to be 2½".) Trim the binding ends to the marked points, and then sew the ends together with a diagonal seam. ②

Trim the excess fabric from the joined strip, leaving a ¼" seam allowance. Then press the seam allowance and stitch this last bit of binding to your project. ③

Fold the binding over the raw edges of your project and hand stitch in place on the back side.

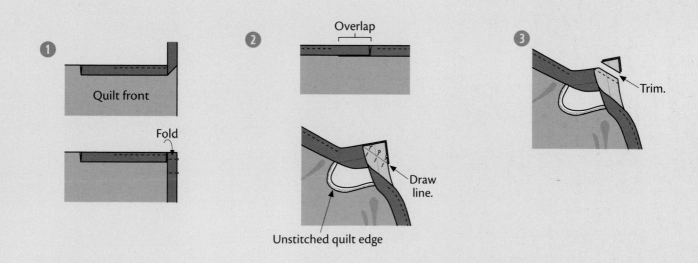

① Quilt front / Fold

② Overlap / Draw line. / Unstitched quilt edge

③ Trim.

Blanket Stitch

Start with a knotted thread and hide it under an appliqué piece. Bring the needle up in the background fabric at the edge of the appliqué piece. Working from left to right, insert the needle down into the appliqué and bring it back up along the edge at a right angle to the edge as shown. The thread should be underneath the needle point. Continue stitching along the appliqué, keeping the stitch length consistent with the distance between the stitches. ④

Buttonhole Stitch

The buttonhole stitch is just like the blanket stitch, but the stitches are worked next to each other, without any space between. ⑤

Clipping Curves and Points

When sewing together parts of a project that involve curves, it's much easier to make a nice, smooth seam if you clip into the seam allowance along the curved edges. For inner points make a snip into the seam allowance before turning the pieces right side out. Trim corners, such as on a rectangular or square pillow, before turning, for nice, flat corners. When you press the piece with the right sides out, the seam allowances will be able to splay open and lie flat. ⑥

Edgestitching and Topstitching

Some projects in this book use edgestitching or topstitching or both to help secure finished edges and make them lie flat and look neat. Edgestitching is done close to the edge of a fabric piece, as the name implies. Try to sew ⅛" or less from the edge. This is often called for when a narrow (⅛" or ¼") edge has been turned under.

Topstitching is generally done ¼" from the edge of the fabric or ¼" from a row of edgestitching. Topstitching is decorative whereas edgestitching is more functional for securing narrow edges that have been turned under or helping to keep seam allowances in place. Used together, topstitching and edgestitching add extra security, such as on straps of a tote bag, when the project will be subjected to lots of wear and tear. ⑦

④

⑤

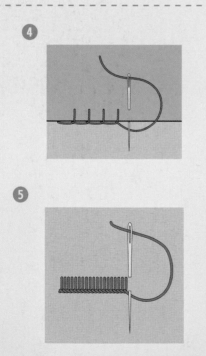

⑥

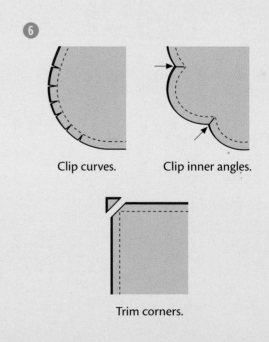

Clip curves.   Clip inner angles.

Trim corners.

Embroidery Stitches

Simple hand-embroidery stitches add extra detail and a very personal touch to your handmade gifts!

French Knot: Knot the thread and come up from underneath to the desired location. Wrap the thread around the needle three times close to the fabric and then reenter the fabric right next to where the thread comes up. Pull the needle through, leaving the knot on the surface of the fabric. ⑧

Stem Stitch: Bring the needle up at A and down at B. Repeat, bringing the needle up at C and down at D. Continue, keeping the thread on the same side of the stitching line. This is a nice stitch for tendrils and vines. ⑨

Fat Eighth and Fat Quarter

These are cuts of fabric that are popular with quilters. A fat eighth measures 9" x 21", as opposed to a ⅛-yard piece that measures 4½" x 42". A fat quarter measures 18" x 21", compared to a ¼-yard piece that measures 9" x 42".

Felting Wool

Wool needs to be felted before using it to prevent it from fraying. Hand-dyed wool has already been washed, but if wool comes straight off the bolt, you'll need to wash it. The fabric must be close to 100% wool for the felting process to work. If it contains other fibers, it won't felt evenly. Wool will shrink 20% to 30% when felted, so if your wool hasn't already been felted, start with at least 30% more than you need, to allow for shrinking.

Felting is easiest to do in a washing machine—it's a combination of the water temperature and agitation that felts the wool. Use a touch of detergent to loosen the fibers. Wash the wool in hot water with a cold-water rinse and a lot of agitation. If the wool is felted enough, allow to air dry. If you want it thicker, dry in a hot dryer, checking it periodically so that you don't felt it too much. If it is not felted enough, repeat the washing process again.

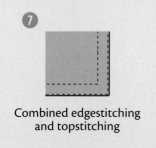

Combined edgestitching and topstitching

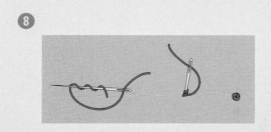

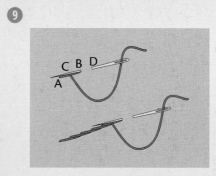

Fusible Appliqué

Fusible web provides a quick-and-easy way to adhere one fabric layer on top of another. Trace the shape you want to appliqué onto the paper side of the fusible web. Cut the shape out loosely. Following the manufacturer's instructions, iron the adhesive side of the web to the wrong side of the appliqué fabric, cut out the shape on the drawn lines, and then iron it onto the background fabric. To minimize stiffness from the adhesive, you can cut away the center of the fusible-web shape before fusing it to the appliqué fabric. ⑩

Decorative machine stitching (such as a blanket stitch or satin stitch) can be worked around the appliqué edges to make this type of appliqué quite durable—a good feature for pillows and quilts that will be laundered. As an alternative, the edges can be left unstitched on projects that won't be exposed to a lot of wear and tear, such as a wall hanging.

Layering and Basting a Quilt

After the quilt top is done, press it carefully and mark it for quilting if desired. Layer it with batting and backing to create the quilt "sandwich." Cut the backing and backing 4" to 6" longer and wider than the quilt top.

⑩
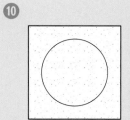
Trace pattern.

Cut loosely around shape and cut out center.

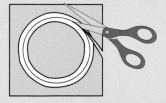
Fuse to wrong side of appliqué fabric and cut on the drawn line.

Spread the backing out on a clean, flat surface. Anchor it with masking tape to keep it slightly taut and wrinkle-free. Spread the batting over the backing, smoothing out any wrinkles. Center the quilt top over the layers.

Begin in the center and baste the layers together using rustproof safety pins for machine quilting or a needle and thread for hand quilting. Work diagonally to each corner and then baste a grid of horizontal and vertical lines 6" to 8" apart. Baste around the edges. ⑪

Pressing

When pressing seam allowances, lift the iron before moving it, rather than gliding it back and forth over the fabric. This makes the fabric less likely to become distorted and it keeps your seam allowances from getting caught up in the edge of the iron. ⑫

When pressing pieces involving fusible web, use a pressing cloth on top of the project to prevent the iron from becoming gummy. A nonstick appliqué pressing sheet can be used to layer and compose appliqués before fusing them to the background.

When pressing delicate fabrics such as wool or silk, use a press cloth over them to prevent scorching.

Satin Stitching

Machine satin stitching is one way to secure the edges of fusible appliqué. Use it when your project will get a lot of use or be washed often. Set your machine to a zigzag stitch (make sure you have an appropriate presser foot in place) and set the stitch width and length to slightly shorter and narrower than the standard setting. Sew around the appliqué shape with one swing of the needle stitching into the appliqué shape and the other swing stitching into the background fabric. ⑬

Seam Allowances

In quiltmaking, seam allowances are typically ¼" wide. In garment sewing, the standard is ⅝". In this book, we've used ¼" seam allowances for patchwork, but sometimes we've used ½" seam allowances on projects that may be subjected to more stress, such as tote bags, or those that have more bulk, such as sweaters or jeans. If not specified, use a ¼" seam allowance.

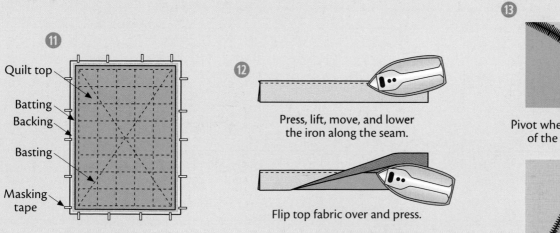

⑪ Quilt top / Batting / Backing / Basting / Masking tape

⑫ Press, lift, move, and lower the iron along the seam.

Flip top fabric over and press.

⑬ Pivot.

Pivot when needle is outside of the appliqué shape.

Use a narrower zigzag at points.

Cassie Barden has been making art her whole life, from painting, filmmaking, and digital illustration to making odd stuffed animals and wild costumes for Burning Man. Inspired by everything from Japanese fashion and classic cartoons to contemporary art and design, she loves living a creative life where there is always something new to explore. Taught by her mom to sew when she was a kid, Cassie began designing her own patterns after college and published her first book, *The New Handmade*, with Martingale & Company in 2008. The sequel, *Everyday Handmade*, coauthored with her friend Adrienne Smitke, was released in 2011. Cassie pursues art and sewing full time from the home she shares with her boyfriend in Seattle.

After seeing the beautiful quilts made by family members, **Sarah Bisel** knew she wanted to make her own kind of quilts. Now, as a mother of four young children, she loves making quilts for her sweet kiddos as well as for other loved ones. Designing and sewing quilts gives Sarah the artistic boost she needs to stay sane and happy. Sarah's greatest ambition is to convert others to the love of quiltmaking! With her book, *Fast, Flirty, and Fun* (Martingale & Company, 2010), she's off to a great start. Check out Sarah's blog at www.milkandhoney designs.blogspot.com.

Kim Brackett lives in Florida with her husband and three cats. She began quilting in 1988, but didn't finish her first quilt until 10 years later! Kim works full-time as a paralegal and enjoys designing and making scrap quilts in her spare time. She has authored two books for Martingale, *Scrap-Basket Surprises* (2009) and

Scrap-Basket Sensations (2011). You can visit Kim's blog at www.magnoliabay quilts.blogspot.com.

Jenny Wilding Cardon has been designing since high school, where she would create eccentric clothing and make her friends wear it to class. She is the author of *ReSew: Turn Thrift-Store Finds into Fabulous Designs* (2011) and *The Little Box of Baby Quilts* (2007). Her designs have also been published in several quilt magazines. Jenny writes about her sewing, thrifting, and family life at WildCards (www.thewildcards.com).

Vanessa Christenson sewed her first stitch 10 years ago and hasn't stopped since. She creates things on a daily basis just to make room in her head for the next batch of ideas to move in. She currently finds herself living in rural America with her husband of 13 years, four kids, a dog, and a cat. You can find her projects and musings at www.VanessaChristenson.com.

Inspired by simple shapes and bright colors, **Karen Clifton** uses new and up-cycled wool, beads, and her imagination to create one-of-a-kind presents that are fun and functional. Karen believes that making handcrafted gifts is a great way to have fun, play with and combine different materials, and spend time connecting with your inner artist.

Linda Lum DeBono loves color. It infuses all of her designs, from quilts to knits to papercrafts. Recently, she's indulged her passion for color in a fabric line with Henry Glass & Co. In addition to designing fabric and publishing patterns, Linda has authored several books and had her

designs featured in *American Patchwork & Quilting* and *Quilts and More*. See her website for additional information: www.lindalumdebono.com.

After she won a national challenge with just the third quilt she'd ever made, **Kim Diehl's** newfound hobby quickly blossomed into a full-time career. In addition to designing quilts and authoring her "Simple" series of books for Martingale & Company, Kim has designed several fabric collections for Henry Glass & Co. She travels nationally sharing her quilts and teaching her easy techniques.

Sara Diepersloot has had a passion for sewing and design since she was a young girl. That passion led to a degree in fashion design and pattern making, and she worked in the fashion industry for several years before starting her family. These days, Sara is a full-time mom of four, chauffeur, cook, and homework helper in addition to being the author of *Simple Style: Easy Weekend Quilts* (Martingale & Company, 2009).

Mary V. Green learned to sew as a child and taught herself to knit and crochet as a teenager, but she didn't discover quiltmaking until she was in her early 30s. Although she appreciates contemporary quilts, she *loves* traditional designs. The humble Nine Patch—the first block she ever made—is still her favorite, its many variations providing endless design possibilities.

Barbara Groves and Mary Jacobson of "Me and My Sister Designs" have had their hands in almost every aspect of the creative crafting industry. These sisters and one-time shop owners have expanded their love of quilting and crafting into a business that now includes designing fabrics for Moda, developing the SideWinder portable bobbin winder, and producing designs for their many patterns and books. Visit them at www.meandmysisterdesigns.com.

Beth Kovich, a textile/fiber junkie extraordinaire, is no stranger to the world of quilting and sewing. She has had numerous quilts featured in Martingale & Company publications and is the coauthor of *Snuggle Up: 8 Lap Quilts to Warm Your Home* (2002). Beth is the creative design force behind Wicked Wool, a popular online business that focuses on primitive rug hooking, original designs, and hand-dyed wool (www.wickedwool. com). New endeavors include raising heritage-breed Black Cotswold sheep and a happy flock of chickens with her family in the Pacific Northwest.

Cindy Lammon has been quilting since 1981, when the birth of her first child kept her home and in need of a creative pursuit. After trying other types of needlework, she found quilting to be the perfect fit. As a passion for quilting developed, so did the desire to start designing quilts. She currently has three books published with Martingale & Company: *Gathered From the Garden* (2008), *Flower Pots* (2009), and *Flowers All Around* (2010). Visit Cindy at www.hyacinthquiltdesigns. blogspot.com.

Cheryl Lynch has been making gifts for family and friends since she was a teenager. Nothing is more rewarding for her than coming up with the perfect idea. With each stitch, she thinks of the recipient and the smile it will bring. Cheryl fell in love with wool appliqué after seeing antique penny rugs. Wool is a very forgiving textile, and you don't have to worry about fraying edges. She likes to say "it's like stitching through butter."

Kay Mackenzie's teapot design came to her right away when the idea of sewing the perfect gift came up. Kay has designed a number of teapot appliqué patterns, and she has often heard quilters say that they're inspired to make something special for a friend who collects teapots. Kay is also the author of *Easy Appliqué Blocks: 50 Designs in 5 Sizes* (2009) and *Inspired by Tradition: 50 Appliqué Blocks in 5 Sizes* (2011) from Martingale & Company. Visit www. kaymackenzie.com to see all of her appliqué designs.

As one-half of the design team Joined at the Hip, **Avis Shirer** is known for primitive, whimsical designs. She loves to accent her appliqué and patchwork with wool, rickrack, buttons, and more. Avis and her design partner, Tammy Johnson, have published 12 books and more than 200 patterns. Visit Avis at www.joinedat thehip.com.

Adrienne Smitke grew up in a house full of handmade quilts and clothes. Her mother taught her to sew at an early age, even once assigning her sewing "homework" over summer vacation. She made a rad pair of black and neon green shorts (it was the '80s, after all). Drawing on her creative childhood, Adrienne studied illustration and graphic design in college, during which she finally began experimenting with sewing again on her own. She coauthored her first book, *Everyday Handmade,* with her friend Cassie Barden, published by Martingale & Company (2011). You can see more of her patterns in *A Baker's Dozen* (2010) and *Jelly Babies* (2011), also from Martingale & Company.

Karen Costello Soltys is a knitting, rug-hooking, quilting, movie-watching, reading, backyard chicken-raising enthusiast. When not pursuing those interests, she works at Martingale & Company as its

managing editor. Karen is the author of *Bits and Pieces: 18 Small Quilts from Fat Quarters and Scraps* (2009) and has designed projects for numerous other books, including *Hooked on Wool, A Baker's Dozen,* and *Jelly Babies* (Martingale & Company, 2006, 2010, and 2011, respectively).

Cheryl Almgren Taylor is a fabric-addicted quilter with a passion for appliqué. She is the author of *Deck the Halls* (Martingale & Company, 2009), and *Inspirational Appliqué* (2011). Her work has been featured in *McCall's Quilting* and *McCall's Quick Quilts*. She has been on the faculty at International Quilt Festival in Houston and Long Beach, and she travels regionally and nationally to teach and lecture. When not quilting, she spends her time as a public-school teacher, a pastor's wife, and a long-distance grandma.

If **Cynthia Tomaszewski** was a cocktail, she'd be called "Traditional with a Twist." She loves traditional designs and fabrics, but enjoys making them uniquely "today" with the added use of embellishments such as beads, buttons, sequins, tassels, and threads. Cynthia, like you, loves to share her passion for needlework with family and friends, and what better way than with small, handmade gifts. Visit Cynthia on her website at www. simpleas.com or her blog at www.moon goddessuae.blogspot.com.

Shelley Wicks and Jeanne Large are busy ladies who not only design and market their own unique line of "Urban Country" patterns, but they also own and operate The Quilt Patch, a warm and welcoming shop in Moose Jaw, Saskatchewan, Canada. Shelley and Jeanne are the coauthors of two books with Martingale and are looking forward to having their very first fabric collection hit the market very soon! Check out their website: www.thequiltpatch.ca.

You might also enjoy these other fine titles from

Martingale & Company

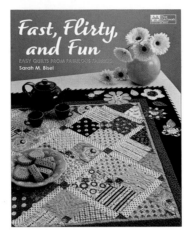

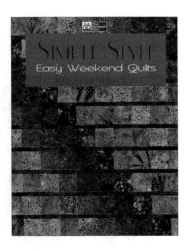

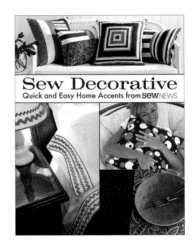

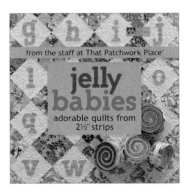

Our books are available at bookstores and your favorite craft, fabric, and yarn retailers.
Visit us at www.martingale-pub.com or contact us at:

1-800-426-3126
International: 1-425-483-3313
Fax: 1-425-486-7596
Email: info@martingale-pub.com

Martingale®
& C O M P A N Y

America's Best-Loved Craft & Hobby Books®
America's Best-Loved Knitting Books®

America's Best-Loved Quilt Books®